MW01289170

Empath -

2 in 1 A Comprehensive Guide for Emotional Healing, Self-Protection & Survival for Empaths and Highly Sensitive People

Featuring – Empath Healing (Vol.1) & Empath (Vol.2)

by

Marianne Gracie

© Copyright 2017 by Marianne Gracie

All rights reserved.

The following book is reproduced below with the goal of providing information that is as accurate and reliable as possible. Regardless, purchasing this book can be seen as consent to the fact that both the publisher and the author of this book are in no way experts on the topics discussed within and that any recommendations or suggestions that are made herein are for entertainment purposes only. Professionals should be consulted as needed prior to undertaking any of the action endorsed herein.

This declaration is deemed fair and valid by both the American Bar Association and the Committee of Publishers Association and is legally binding throughout the United States.

Furthermore, the transmission, duplication or reproduction of any of the following work including specific information will be considered an illegal act irrespective of if it is done electronically or in print. This extends to creating a secondary or tertiary copy of the work or a recorded copy and is only allowed with express written consent from the Publisher. All additional right reserved.

The information in the following pages is broadly considered to be a truthful and accurate account of facts and as such any inattention, use or misuse of the information in question by the reader will render any resulting actions solely under their purview. There are no scenarios in which the publisher or the original author of this work can be in any fashion deemed liable for any hardship or damages that may befall them after undertaking information described herein.

Additionally, the information in the following pages is intended only for informational purposes and should thus be thought of as universal. As befitting its nature, it is presented without assurance regarding its prolonged validity or interim quality. Trademarks that are mentioned are done without written consent and can in no way be considered an endorsement from the trademark holder.

Table of Contents

Empath Healing (Vol.1)

Empath Healing (Vol.2)

Preface

Dear Reader,

Thank you for taking the time to purchase this title. I would like to share a quick word before you start reading further. This title was released in the hope of helping empaths come to terms with and overcome their past hurts and traumas. As empaths, we are prone to deeper emotional and psychological wounding compared to our non-empathic counterparts. This doesn't mean there is anything wrong with us, but that we just need to take the time to heal our pain. Once we heal we step into our true power and can learn to share our gift with the world, to not only empower other people's lives but our own as well. It is my hope that the reader can achieve this lofty ideal and with the information provided help keep themselves guarded against any future hurts. I, myself, was born with the gift of heightened sensitivity, so have written this from my own personal experiences and through working with my clients. Learning from other people's struggles and stories can give us the strength to endure our own. I sincerely hope you can begin to change your life and that this book offers you some practical ways to do so.

Thank you!

Marianne Gracie (Author)

P.S. – Feel free to download my free True Self-Healing Meditation here if you wish.

Introduction

If you are reading this book, I am assuming that you either know you are an Empath, you're still trying to figure it out or know someone who is. Either way, you have come to the right place to help expand your knowledge as this book contains the most up to date information available on the subject.

The very first thing anyone who is interested in this topic should come to understand, is that this trait is part of an empaths genetic make-up. It will be with them for their whole life. It was likely inherited from one or even both parents. It is not an illness, disease or psychological disorder which can be treated by medicine or therapy.

But do not worry, you're not alone. Statistics have pointed out that around 1 in 20 people are also empaths or highly sensitive individuals. If you're an empath and have picked up this book to find a solution to this 'condition', then I am afraid you won't find one. With that said, the purpose of this book is to teach the empath exactly how to manage this trait effectively so they can reap the benefits of this gift while creating a happier future for themselves.

Along with empaths, there is another group of people who are commonly called Highly Sensitive People (HSP). For the purpose of this book, these two terms will be used interchangeably. Although I do understand some believe there is a difference between the two. The knowledge in this book will work for either Empaths or HSP's. Both types possess a heightened sense of feeling. That is the basis of which this book tackles the topic of feeling and sensitivity. So, do not be put off if you have classified yourself as a different term, this book provides information and knowledge for a range of related subjects.

The main purpose of this book is to help people begin to see that this attribute is a gift to the world and not a hindrance. Unfortunately, we have never been shown how to harness this attribute and work with it. Like anything in life, when we don't fully understand something, it can leave us feeling confused or fearful.

Having grown up with this trait and always feeling different from others, I have personally experienced many lows. It was only until I realized that I had to learn more about myself and how to accept all parts of me, that I was able to harness the true power which resides in being an Empath. Now I see it as special gift, something which many others do not have and can never have. Learning how to use this trait has enabled me to have and experience better relationships because I can understand others better without getting caught up in their emotions (something I struggled with most of my life).

Before this, I would often be left feeling drained from other people and certain environments I found myself in. After eventually becoming tired of being dragged down, I spent many years living alone so I wouldn't have to face the energy drainage of others. But, over time I realized that cutting myself of like this, wasn't beneficial for me or the world. I had a gift which I should be sharing and empowering others with. So I began to work, study and learn new ways I could go out into the world as a strong empath and use my abilities for good.

After a short time of educating myself, I discovered tools and techniques which would help me to thrive. I learnt ways to hold my energy so I could go out into the world and not be overwhelmed by others. This in turn, would allow me to make better decisions and experience less anxiety, which ultimately lead to a more fulfilled life.

How effectively we can connect with others, is one of the main factors of how much happiness we will experience in life. I agree, that empaths may be at a disadvantage at the beginning but from my own experience and other people I have worked with, what seems like a disability can be transformed into an incredible gift, with which empaths are able to connect with others much more effectively than most people can. Empathy is a communication tool, which allows us to become great communicators by understanding others on a much deeper level. Learning how to work with this will open so many doors for you.

This title will start by looking at empaths and the problems they face in greater detail. With these new understandings, we are able uncover emotional pain from years of living in this way. This wounding must be healed first if we are to move forward and positively impact the future of our lives. Here we will look at various methods of healing and overcoming past traumas. Along with this, the book contains a survival guide about all the tools empaths have at their disposal to be able to function at their best, while keeping anxiety, negativity and fear at bay. Many of the practical exercises in this book have been broken down in easy to understand chucks which can be implemented almost immediately.

The other facets empaths and sensitives must deal with are overwhelming environments such as crowded places and the energy of the planet. With so much negativity in the world, empaths must find a way to rise above it. In our inner journey of learning how to conquer and harness this natural feeling ability, we become accustomed and prepared to help tackle the problems people are facing in our world. An empaths life mission therefore, is of the highest purpose. Never forget this, it's this very reason that will help keep you strong!

What is an Empath?

Empathy – the capability to understand another's emotions.

Everyone is empathic, we all have a natural ability to feel, understand and relate to others. It is what makes us human and is a natural part of our hereditary make-up. Empathy is identifying with the other person, but everyone experiences varying degrees of this. Some people feel very little empathy, these people can suffer from psychological disorders such as sociopaths and psychopaths. Feeling a healthy degree of empathy is normal and a benchmark of a balanced personality. However, empaths are on the higher end of the spectrum - they feel too much, this makes the trait difficult to manage. Without knowing how to handle it, they can often be left feeling overwhelmed by their surroundings, particularly social situations or crowded places. They tend to overly-identify with people they come into contact with because they unconsciously pickup too much energy and emotion from them. This can become incredibly draining and not to mention very confusing, as they feel what others are feeling.

At the most fundamental level, everything in the world, living or otherwise, is made of energy. Each type of energy has a certain vibrational frequency. An empath has a sophisticated psychic ability to emotionally tune into the energetic experience of other people, certain places and even animals.

Empaths and HSP's can often pick-up on what others are thinking even before anything is said due to this natural sensitivity. Their skills go further than this however, as they are also great at reading others through body language, tone of voice, movements and thoughts, these abilities give them the natural skills to become great communicators.

Empaths sense and feel unseen energies of any situation or experience. For example, they may enter a room where an argument has just taken place and will often feel the presence of a foul energy. They can detect this through the energetic residue left in the room from the argument, this promotes their innate ability of natural intuitiveness. Often unconsciously, sensitives will experience good or bad vibes about a person or place. They also possess a natural creative flair, which they can express in various forms through their great imaginations and natural charisma, this is what draws others towards them.

From all these listed benefits, it might sound like being an Empath is ideal and something everyone should aspire too, but unfortunately all these positive attributes are balanced with some not so desirable qualities.

A sensitive person feels much more deeply than someone who doesn't have this natural tendency. Empathic people can be so sensitive, that they often unconsciously absorb others energies into their own bodies, this causes them to feel other people's emotions very deeply. Because of this, they often become confused and struggle to identify their own emotional needs and wants, as they're so overwhelmed by other people's feelings. This translates into the natural skills of nurturing and listening with compassion, consideration and a deep understanding of others. They are able to feel others pain and understand them more deeply because they've had a direct experience of their emotions. This attracts people to them, like a moth to a flame, people will often leave an interaction with an empath feeling much better. Animals are also naturally drawn to the energy of empaths.

Sensitive people are usually the ones, whom their friends turn to for help and advice. They will often go out of their way to help others and sacrifice their own needs in the process. For these reasons, it is incredibly important that empaths discover ways to protect themselves from taking on too much energy from others. People who 'dump' their negativity onto empaths, usually sense on some level that they feel better after speaking to an empath. Therefore, they continue to do it, it can almost become a form of psychic abuse. A major downside of having heightened empathic abilities is the development of weak or non-existent boundaries, finding it hard to say no because they've taken on others pain as their own.

HSPs and empaths can struggle to notice the difference between physical stress and energetic stress. For instance, when they have to make an effort to be more sociable this tends to tire them out physically because they're constantly bombarded with energetic stimulus from all around, it takes longer to process everything coming in. You may often feel worn out from meeting many new people at once or from being exposed to a new place or environment.

All words hold an energetic pattern, this frequency is taken on by the person who is speaking, reading or thinking these words. Words contain a meaning for us and each one carries a comparable emotional signature. When certain words are spoken they naturally evoke an emotional response. For example, strong words such as love and hate, contain within them the energetic meaning of the word. The person who therefore, is reading, thinking or talking about love, adds their emotion to the already powerful word. An empath can pick up on this subtle energy even though it wasn't the speakers intention. They're so naturally attuned to their energetic atmosphere that they cannot help but feel everything.

Empaths have so much power that they need to find ways in which to harness it by first learning to shield and protect themselves from unwanted energies. Once this goal is attained they are able to go out into the world in a bubble of protection and do amazing work to help heal and lift the planet to a higher vibration.

Sensitives can be found throughout the world, among all cultures and religions. In some cases, they can be found living alone, in a very quiet, depressed or neurotic lifestyle. Becoming a loner is an easy way out. Without learning how to protect their space, some are forced to live alone as being around others is just too tiresome and draining. So they like to spend time in solitude and nature can become a favorite ally. Here they find that the Earth is naturally grounding and recharges their overstimulated nervous system. Nature therefore becomes a powerful tool in the life of an empath.

Why am I like this?

Many empaths whom I have come into contact with, ask the same question - why have I been lumbered with this trait? In modern society, being extroverted and out-going is seen as something to aspire to and how 'normal' healthy people should behave. But empaths are naturally introverted, so trying to fit the mold of modern society can leave us feeling out of place and thinking there is something inherently wrong with us. It is important to recognize that there is nothing wrong with you and that you're not alone!

For most of my adult life I believed that my sensitivity was something psychological which I had picked up during my childhood. Following this I went through many years of therapy and self-exploration to eventually understand that it wasn't something I was able to get away from. It was a part of me. Genetically hardwired into my entire system. Once we come to this realization, we can then begin to accept and work with it.

Although there hasn't been much physiological research conducted to examine the causes of heightened sensitivity, here is some information to help give you a slightly better understanding of why you are this way. On a biological level, the reason empaths feel more deeply is due to a 'unique variation' in the workings of their central nervous system. Empaths have a much more sensitive nervous system when compared to non-empaths, this is what causes the sensations of being overwhelmed. Our nervous systems are picking up on everything from the environment and people around us. Due to this heightened sensitivity, empaths will also experience physical pain more deeply. As I child, I remember I hated washing my hair because I couldn't stand the water over my head. I couldn't enjoy children's swings and rides because the stimulation was just too much for me to take. I felt everything more deeply, I would even go red in the face through embarrassment very easily. Plain and simple – Empaths feel everything more!

This overly sensitive nervous system is usually genetic and is often passed down from one of the parents. To help improve our understanding of the physical reasons of this phenomenon we will take a brief over view of how the nervous system works and its purpose in helping us function.

The Nervous System

What is it? On a very basic level, it is the control center of our bodies – controlling all physiological and psychological reactions. It is made up of 2 parts – the central and peripheral nervous system. The central nervous system is comprised of the brain and spinal cord. The peripheral nervous system consists of many nerves spread throughout the body which enable us to engage our five senses. These nerves all feed into and are extensions of the central nervous system.

It is the most powerful system of the human body due to its control of our bodily senses, without it we wouldn't be able function. It allows us to feel heat and cold. When we feel hungry, messages are sent via the nerves to our brains to signal we need food. All these external and internal messages are processed by electrical and chemical signals which come to and from our nerve cells.

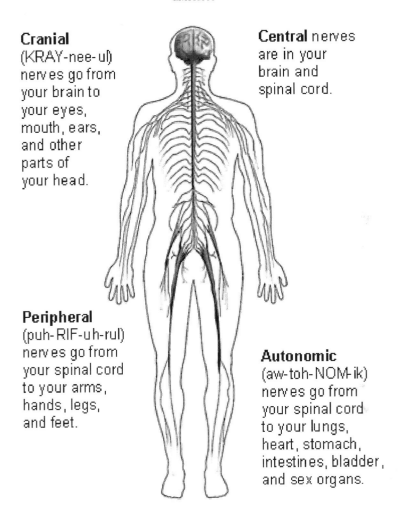

Cranial
(KRAY-nee-ul)
nerves go from
your brain to
your eyes,
mouth, ears,
and other
parts of
your head.

Central nerves
are in your
brain and
spinal cord.

Peripheral
(puh-RIF-uh-rul)
nerves go from
your spinal cord
to your arms,
hands, legs,
and feet.

Autonomic
(aw-toh-NOM-ik)
nerves go from
your spinal cord
to your lungs,
heart, stomach,
intestines, bladder,
and sex organs.

It is not clear whether both the central and peripheral nervous systems are highly sensitized. Or if it is only one part. But as we understand, the peripheral nervous system is responsible for the many nerves which travel throughout the body, this part will most certainly be highly sensitized, as it is what connects us to our reality. It is very likely the brain will also be, especially when we consider, sensitives respond more to certain stimulants and depressants (such as caffeine and alcohol) which work directly on the brain. If you have noticed getting drunk easily or caffeine has a big impact on you then it's extremely likely your brain is highly sensitized also.

In later chapters, we will look at what dietary habits and exercises you can incorporate into your life to help physically calm the nervous system. This should allow you to feel more grounded and more in control of yourself and your environment.

Global Energy

Not only must we begin to work to protect against others energy, who intrude on our boundaries but also protect against global waves of unconscious emotions such as fear, which are produced through negativity. When the negativity on our Planet is high, it is easily picked up by sensitives which can then cause further anxiety, this can make us feel very heavy and have a pounding like effect on us.

It is difficult to quantify when the energetic frequency of the planet is negative since we have no instruments to measure it. But we must use this gift, our sixth sense to sense it. By using our intuition, you can help promote harmony and healing around yourself, your loved ones and the planet.

If for instance, wars or political disputes are on-going, that have divided and created tension between large groups of people, there is no way of avoiding these collective forces of energy. Most people are unconscious of the energy created by large populations of people but empaths can become aware and begin to move themselves above it. This is achieved by protecting ourselves and having a positive impact on the people and environment around us (exactly how to do this will be discussed in later chapters). Empaths are needed on this planet to help balance these negative energies. It can feel like a challenge and we may ask why we have been lumbered with this task but this is the way it is. We can promote positivity on the planet in many ways even through little tasks such as helping others, promoting peace, creating positive content such as videos, blogs, articles and pictures, to name but a few.

Social anxiety and the Empath

Anxiety robs us of vital life energy. This unwanted psychological thought pattern consumes a significant part of our minds energy which we could use more productively to enhance our lives.

Without consciously taking control over themselves, empaths are open to everything. They have no protection. Research has proven that people who suffer from social anxiety are much more exposed to other people's emotional states. This sensitivity causes physical sensations within the body which is referred to as anxiety.

A 2011 study (1) proved people who suffer from social phobias were hypersensitive to other people's mind states and thoughts. The anxiety ridden participants were able to accurately perceive the feelings and thoughts of others in their close vicinity. This essentially proved that empathy is a gift as the volunteers were able to determine others emotional states just from being in their presence.

However, the downside of this psychic gift was that others emotions and energies was so distressing for the participants, that their brains would create anxiety feelings in the body in order to protect itself from what the researchers referred to as 'emotional pollution'. If your anxiety leads to panic attacks this can cause empaths to take on other states in an attempt to keep the panic attacks at bay. These include OCD, not leaving the house and depression, to name but a few.

Other sources of evidence have proven that empathy is impaired or even reduced in people who suffer from depression. This could mean that empaths may unconsciously retreat into depression in an attempt to block their natural empathic abilities. They may see this as the only real solution to stop themselves from being overwhelmed by others and their environment. Depression is effectively a cognitive dissonance, where the suffer denies or represses their own feelings, whether negative or positive. More on this later.

Anxiety – The empaths ability to effortlessly pick up subtle energies and emotions of their environment leaves them overwhelmed by too much extrasensory input. This overload causes people to panic when it becomes too much. The whole system feels like it is being bombarded with information and energy. This creates feelings of inadequacy within us because when we look around and see everyone else functioning fine, it makes us feel like we're the only ones who are so distressed. By seeing others functioning 'normally', we make the assumption that they either feel like we do and are still able to be effective or that they feel different from us, either way this enforces the belief that we must be either weird or strange. This type of thinking sends the message to ourselves that something is inherently wrong with us. Years of this type of programming, is incredibly harmful to an empaths self-esteem.

Empaths will look to the future if they are often left distressed with anxiety which creates more dis-ease since they are being pulled out of the present moment. It is not uncommon to suffer from intense anxiety, with a belief that something bad is going to happen at any moment. Whether they are going out with friends, out shopping, out riding in a car, or wherever it is, they are often accompanied by high levels of fear. Feeling like this essentially takes any pleasure out of living.

An evolved way to begin to look at this problem is first recognizing that these thoughts are not giving us what we need. We must find another healthier way to live. The anxious feelings are coming from our environment and from our unresolved emotional issues which are being expressed through dysfunctional thought patterns. The non-stop over anxious feelings are one big manifestation of all our fears which need to be purged. All anxiety and negative feelings need to be processed. When there is so much ego energy and self-loathing in others, like with the general unconscious population, this is easily picked up and transferred to sensitives.

I used to trick myself into believing that my anxious feelings were keeping me safe and without them I would end up in fearful circumstances. I would make logical arguments to myself to justify feeling worried all of the time. In the end, what I discovered was that I lacked belief in myself. If I had a healthy sense of self-esteem then no matter what life presented me with, I would be able to handle it because I was competent and capable. These positive beliefs can only come from a healthy sense of self-esteem and confidence. That is why self-love crushes any type of anxiety, if gives us the belief we can handle life.

For empaths who are familiar with the law of attraction, it is important to understand that when we are full of fear and anxious, then vibrationally we are unable to attract the things we want into our lives. We only bring in what matches our vibration. It is of no surprising then if it sometimes feels like we are struggling to move forward. We must change ourselves first before our world can reflect this back to us. Living in fear, anxiety and worry will only bring more of this into our lives. The hard truth is that empaths will find it more challenging to change since they must deal with not only their own issues, but the compounded burden of over stimulation. Of course, this makes it more difficult, but at the same time, much more worthwhile. The high empaths can feel once they have conquered themselves is unparalleled.

Intimacy Problems

Intimacy is the basis of close relationships. It essentially means allowing another to get close enough to us, to see all of our darkest secrets and flaws. Sharing our emotional feelings with another creates an emotional bond between us. This can only be achieved by letting go of and releasing any defenses which we had previously held in place to help keep us safe.

Experiencing true intimacy can be incredibly challenging for many people. But none more so than for Empaths. This word intimacy has been famously broken down into the phrase *'Into me you see'*. When we take into account all the pain and heartbreak we have had to endure through life it is easier to understand why being seen closely 'warts and all' can be so terrifying.

In defense of being exposed to others, we put up walls to protect us, but these walls shut off our feelings and keep our true self hidden away. These walls can take form through various methods such as attracting the wrong partners, avoiding close relationships or becoming a social outcast, a loner. We often convince ourselves that we are doing the right thing but our resulting actions usually come from a place of fear. The fear that our deepest flaws will be exposed and we will be seen as inadequate.

It is not uncommon that empaths will remain single their whole life, since they like to be alone so much as they don't have to feel others stresses and emotions. Often times they become so accustomed to spending time alone that they don't feel lonely anymore but this is not incredibly healthy. Empaths should understand that they are capable of healthy relationships providing respectful boundaries can be established between partners.

To achieve this we must learn to make ourselves vulnerable again and trust that we are equipped enough to deal with whatever comes our way. This is the mark of the fully mature person.

In an authentically intimate relationship, all of our fears can be brought out into the light of love and be examined. This is one of the greatest benefits of relationships, they allow us to share ourselves with another and grow together. When there is little genuine intimacy within a relationship then self-doubts and insecurities can creep in, these effectively put the partnership under immense strain. Romantic relationships have a knack of exposing our deepest flaws and insecurities but instead of running from them, we need to hold and understand them to eventually free ourselves.

Healthy intimacy also comes from learning to look within ourselves, *'Into me I see'*. When we develop the courage to truly look at ourselves we learn to gradually accept our fears and faults. This in turn allows us to let others closer. By befriending ourselves, we can then befriend others. Intimacy is also the foundation of social relations, without it there is no real spark when meeting new people. Yes, the people you meet will probably feel comfortable unloading all of their issues onto you, because of your empathic nature, but a genuine connection will remain elusive without a real emotional bond.

This rings true for all our relationships. For example, I have a son and I always had the sense that I wasn't fully connecting with him. He is also an empath, this wasn't something I had discussed with him until he was much older but I was able to see how it had passed down from me to him. I could see it in his traits and behaviors. He is so kind and caring to others. Never any trouble to anyone and like many other empaths, he spends a lot of time on his own. But once I was able to open up and get deeply in touch with my own reservoir of feelings, I was able to get in contact with his feelings. Our children need to feel an emotional connection from us. This is how they learn to get in touch with their own feelings. This will determine if our children will go onto live happy successful lives. Once they feel our deep unconditional love for them, it allows them to open up.

Unfortunately intimacy isn't something which can be found overnight, it comes to us gradually by learning to let go of any resistance and fears by softly opening up to our self and others. Doing this slowly will begin to move you into the right direction for healthy growth and relationships. Start this process by learning to accept yourself just as you are, right now.

Empaths and Intimacy

Empaths often suffer problems in maintaining healthy relationships. I believe this is down to our heightened sensing ability. As children, our feelings were felt too deeply and this was overwhelming or even painful for us. To protect ourselves from these heavy emotions we closed ourselves off out of fear of experiencing pain again. But by blocking out the painful feelings, we obstructed our positive feelings at the same time. The human mind is not logical, it doesn't understand good and bad. If we decide to block our painful feelings, the mind is unable to differentiate between what we want and don't want.

Repression, requires a lot of our psychological energy and we end up blocking much more than just the unwanted stuff but other rich aspects of our personalities too. For instance, by repressing our desire to be seen, we may also lose a natural talent to communicate well. It is almost impossible to only repress one facet of ourselves and avoid others because our traits and feelings are interconnected. If you repress one aspect of yourself, you will inevitably push others away also.

Learning to repress themselves from a young age, sends the young empath within and often into shyness especially if they've experienced too much pain. Then out of fear of feeling again, the empath creates further psychological blocks to help protect themselves.

Life is often even more difficult for the youngster if they grew up in a dysfunctional household witnessing physical, emotional or mental abuse. All of this combined negative energetic stimulus forces the empath to close themselves off from a very young age. As they grow up, they often struggle to reach out and connect with others because of the defense mechanisms they developed earlier in life. Their heightened sensitivity increases any painful feelings, which are almost unbearable for a young child. So, their true self goes into hiding.

I grew up with two sisters in a somewhat dysfunctional family. I do believe my sisters have a certain degree of sensitivity also, but not to the degree which I always have. Anything which happens in the household, is felt and picked up more by the most sensitive child, so the long-term impact they have to deal with is greater too. Empaths feel all experiences much deeper. But, by becoming aware of your natural tendencies you can work to protect and better equip yourself from future psychological and emotional damage. With that said, the painful wounds of childhood will need healing also.

By pushing their feelings and their needs for emotional connection away, these are repressed down into the unconscious psyche. Repression of any feelings doesn't mean that is the end of them. Since all emotions are energy, they cannot be destroyed but only converted. Repressed emotions then come out in other ways, often as anxiety, stress or depression. Our feelings serve to guide us through life which helps give us direction and purpose. By cutting them off is almost like going through life blind, metaphorically speaking. These people will instead look outside of themselves for guidance because they're incapable of trusting their own feelings.

The solution to overcoming these issues, is to stop repressing your feelings while understanding it is safe for you to come out into the world by getting in touch with your emotions, desires and wants – Your true self! It is ok for you to have desires and needs, it is also perfectly acceptable to get these needs met just as much as anyone else's. Other people's needs should not gain priority over yours just because you feel theirs as well. That is what being a healthy mature adult is, owning your own feelings and getting your needs met. This can feel foreign to an empath at the beginning, but it is the first steps to taking ownership back of your Self.

If you have been spending a lot of time alone. You may be repressing your desire to truly connect with others in a healthy way. Human beings are social creatures and always have been. No matter how shut off we sometimes feel, creating connections with others will often be the most fulfilling parts of our lives.

'Relationships are the hallmark of the mature person' – *Brain Tracy* (Motivational Speaker) (2)

Since empaths learn from a young age to sit on their feelings, overtime they become masters at hiding how they feel without even knowingly realizing it. They're unconsciously still under the assumption that if they let someone close, the pain will be unbearable. But, we are grown now. We are not defenseless little children anymore and although we still feel deeply, we can handle and manage the pain better now due to our increased maturity, intellect, reasoning, education and life experiences.

It is ok to have needs. It is ok to have feelings. Let them out, allow yourself to experience them once again. Start to feel yourself again, is there pain there? What do you feel? (There is an exercise later which will take you through this whole process).

Close relationships leave empaths open to more hurt because they'll also pick-up their partners pain. Effectively doubling the heart ache. That is why being in a relationship with a partner who carries emotional wounding can hold the empath back from freeing themselves. In this scenario, they will energetically pick up their partner's pain, this is unavoidable due to the close proximity and connection they share. Then trying to clear and heal your own wounds becomes increasingly difficult.

The flip-side of this, is that empaths have the profound ability to feel love deeper than others. Feeling another's love can transform their whole lives. But first they must pluck up the courage and allow themselves to become vulnerable. The possibility of being able to feel genuine love from another should be the light which empaths follow, this will keep them warm on this frightening journey. The love you will feel at the end of this road will be worth the pain. Until you experience it, you will never know just how profound true love can feel for you.

Sexual Intimacy

Without genuine intimacy, sexual relationships suffer. A healthy emotional connection is the foundation of healthy sexual intimacy. This is why empaths often struggle with sexual dysfunction. We will now briefly look at some sexual issues which can be common in empaths.

Promiscuity - This involves having many casual sexual partners with no real intimate connection. It is not uncommon for empaths to fall under this category due to a lack of self-worth, they try to seek it through having sex with multiple partners. By behaving in this way, they feel some control over their lives as they can choose and control who they have sex with, this gives them a skewed sense of validation of their own worth. They also look for this validation from over performing sexually and then receiving compliments from their partners. This type of behavior can become incredibly addictive and the empath can start to derive all of their self-worth on their sexuality and therefore define themselves through this medium. This can lead to them boasting to others about their sexual prowess. Any such encounters are often followed by intense bouts of shame. On the opposite end of the scale, some empaths can move towards celibacy. Delving into deeper empathic sexual issues is beyond the scope of this book but it is worth remembering that this part of an empaths life is not always straight forward.

Once empaths can begin to feel the intensity of genuine non-physical intimacy it will usually be more profound than anything they had previously experienced physically. Sex is typically the closet an empath can come to another, but this physical closeness doesn't always translate to emotional closeness. This often leaves them feeling rather confused but being truly intimate is much deeper than just having sex. People generally feel sex is the closet they can get to another. But there are levels of deeper intimacy and sex which most people have never experienced, empathic or not.

For empaths to begin honoring themselves and their feelings, they should start becoming more protective of who they decide to share their sexual energy with. Since they want to give and help others, they can sometimes feel that giving sex is all they have to give. If you're an empath who's in a relationship, start to work on emotionally connecting with your partner more and put sex on the back-burner. Or, if dating a new partner, make them wait before you decide to have sex, although this can be difficult for empaths to do. Also, in modern day culture if people are not forth coming with their sexuality in relationships this is seen as something negative. The empaths goal should be to feel and honor themselves first and foremost.

Without genuine intimacy, empaths are unable to connect with their partner on a deeper level, this can often feel like hanging out with a friend as opposed to a being with someone you're deeply in love with. If your relationship feels more like a friendship, or a fake type of intimacy then try to understand this and learn how to deal with it.

The primary emotions include - love, joy, surprise, anger, sadness and fear. Most people are comfortable expressing at least a few of these. Sometimes the negative ones can be more difficult for empaths to get in touch with, especially anger. Since they are so aware and cautious of upsetting others, this can cause them to repress negative emotions such as anger or sadness. Pushing these powerful emotions away creates longer term psychological issues. Empaths often pride themselves on never getting angry. But repressing these feelings is energetically taxing which leads to this energy being expressed in other ways usually through depression, stress or anxiety. When we isolate ourselves from others, we experience the same neuro chemicals in our bodies as when suffering from stress.

Only by getting in touch with yourself will you develop true inner strength, with this you can then begin to tolerate closeness and eventually start to enjoy it. It requires a lot of courage and introspection to really understand if we are in a healthy relationship or not. Being with someone who carries a lot of emotional pain causes a lot of damage to empaths. Although the other person will find it healing and helpful, it can be crippling for a sensitive.

Choosing the Right Partner

Childhood conditioning and past programming's often lead empaths to fall for the wrong person in relationships. But when they start getting more in tune with their self and feelings, the heart and soul naturally begin to align, with this alignment they start to see people who are emotionally available for healthy relationships while steering clear of the abusive and energy draining types. Since we attract what we essentially are, we must become emotionally healthy to have a truly wonderful and fulfilling relationship.

Taking time out from dating and relationships, can be beneficial in helping the empath to develop stronger emotional boundaries. Unfortunately, this won't happen overnight, especially since empaths have weak boundaries through years of letting others emotionally dump on them. Take the time to get in touch with your needs and from there decide what you are looking for from a relationship. Learning to love yourself fully and unconditionally first, will allow you to find someone who mirrors this back to you. This creates the foundation of a healthy intimate relationship. It is in these types of partnerships where the intensity of non-physical intimacy is more powerful than physical intimacy.

By allowing yourself to let go of past hurts you begin healing yourself, this frees you up to start enjoying each moment more and more until eventually you create a great feeling inside yourself, this makes it easier to create healthy connections with others. You are then in a powerful place of being able to consciously select the right partner. Sexual intimacy then becomes the icing on a magnificent cake, and not the whole cake itself.

Although empaths are great at knowing and reading others from their energetic and emotional presence, in close intimate relationships this can become increasingly difficult to do. This is because the emotional connection is sometimes too strong and it distorts the empaths ability to read their partners energy effectively. An empaths' sensing ability is similar to a highly-attuned instrument which works most optimally when others are at a certain emotional range from us. When we allow people too close, this attunement distorts the ability to read the other, which can lead to confusion and misunderstandings. Similar to when the frequency of a radio channel isn't quite tuned in and interference can be heard.

Empaths should learn to take relationships slowly. When they gradually figure the other person out, they can move the relationship to the next level. This creates its own challenges. Not everyone will be willing to take it slow. The partner of an empath must understand that the other person requires a certain amount of time alone. It is also generally believed that empaths have a better relationship with non-empaths as the opposites help to build a stronger partnership. Two empaths together can be a little overwhelming and it can likely be too much for both of them. That is not to suggest that it isn't possible.

Feeling Your Feelings

Here is a technique for getting more in-tune with any repressed feelings you have hidden away for a long time. These can be anxiety related, repressed emotions, or any wants and needs. It includes whatever you have not allowed a healthy expression. Most of the time we aren't even aware of what we repress. Use these processes either in real life situations or while visualizing events. I like to see this exercise as an act of mindful meditation.

1) The first step is to acknowledge the feeling.

When faced with an overwhelming situation which invokes a strong sense of emotion, such as anxiety, pay attention and acknowledge the sensation within your physical body. Whenever we are overcome by emotion this should act as an indicator that there is a potential for inner growth, even though it may make us want to run, flee or attack.

2) Make a conscious choice to stay with the physical sensation.

Do this by taking slow deep breathes, in through the nose and out through the mouth. Stay with the uncomfortable feeling with no resistance and clear mind.

3) Examine the feeling closely.

For example, if you experience nerves while public speaking, using this exercise you can coach yourself out of it. Visualize the event vividly in your mind, feel the bodily sensations you experience when speaking in public. This will cause the body to emotionally react as if the event is happening for real. Take your focus to the part of the body where these feelings of anxiety or discomfort are the most intense. It will usually be in the torso from your throat down to your groin region. Examine the physical sensation, really feel what it feels like. Pay close attention to it and its properties. What color is this feeling? How big is it? How heavy is it? Try to quantify this feeling as much as you can. You can even give it a name. Or call it your buddy, friend or anything which makes the sensation feel less threatening. This allows you to start connecting to and getting to know yourself.

4) Be in absolute non-resistance.

Allow the physical sensations to be, they are neutral, they mean nothing. Forget any thoughts which attach themselves to this feeling. We unconsciously attach thoughts to our feelings which then become our emotions. Instead of feeling the bodily sensation, we instead continually swirl related thoughts around our head over and over, this creates a hormonal response which sends our thoughts into overdrive and creates anxiety. The feeling and the thought have no connection apart from the one we have given it. When the feeling and the thought combine, that is what creates anxiety.

5) Set an intention

Once identifying where in the body this feeling is, set the intention to move it out of you. You can create goals for self-growth or of healing yourself. You can visualize how you will act when these negative feelings have left you.

6) Continue to stay with it for as long as possible while breathing deeply.

Over time the sensation in the body will begin to weaken and the related thoughts will also lessen. Until this happens continue to concentrate and focus intently. Breathe into these feelings. Breathe with them. Each emotion has an energetic signature, this is what you are looking for.

7) Go beyond your comfort zone

The bad feelings we feel, is what most people try to avoid through junk food, alcohol, drugs and TV. Most people cannot face themselves in this way. Overindulgence in anything is what stops us from feeling painful emotions and fears. They want to be processed and expressed but it is painful to do so. The pain of our feelings confronts us when we reach the limits of our comfort zone. Start to pay more attention to this and consciously try to go beyond what is comfortable for you.

8) The key to growth and transmuting old feelings and energies

By consciously pushing ourselves to go further, we delve deeper into our negative feelings. Then by learning to stay with them for long as possible through concentration and focus we eventually move through them. This is called non-resistance.

9) Very strong feelings

When coming across incredibly strong feelings, one thing you can do, is to physically let them out. Grab a pillow and scream into it. Let the feeling out from you. Scream as loud as possible. This screaming can last for a long or short time. Whatever feels right. Sometimes using emotionally moving music can help to move the feeling on. The body will essentially open up to allow the unwanted feelings to finally be processed.

Practice this regularly, on any unwanted emotions. Become more aware and notice what you're feeling in your body whenever you are overcome by a strong sensation or emotion. Try to forget about the thought and just concentrate on the feeling. This is a powerful transformational tool.

The long-term benefits of doing this exercise are immeasurable. The powerful intelligence which resides in unfelt feelings can blossom outward and enrich our mind, which enables us to see life from a brand-new perspective. To keep these feelings trapped, repressed and unprocessed (like we do for many years) comes at a heavy price. The cost was access to our inner gold and self-worth. This gold is a piece of our true self. A piece of our wisdom and inner strength. When we can release these unwanted feelings in a healthy way, we get back a wholeness and intelligence which we have always had, but most likely never experienced.

How to Set Energetic Boundaries

Growing up in a relatively small town I never truly understood just how sensitive I was until later in life (even though I was painfully shy in my youth). My sensitivity was all that I had known and therefore I thought it was normal. In the back of my mind I always felt different from others but I wasn't able to pin-point why this was. When I reached my 30's however, I decided to move to a big city for a brand-new experience. As soon as I set foot into this new place I noticed a huge difference from where I had grown up. I could feel an energetic difference in the atmosphere. It just felt different and I really struggled to settle there. My body always felt on alert and I found it increasingly difficult to relax. For the first six months, I even struggled to sleep, as the energy of the place was much faster paced, then what I had been used to. Also, due to the much higher volumes of people, I couldn't go anywhere where I wasn't surrounded by others. By the end of the day I would feel completely worn out. Even though I would work to keep my own energy high, going out would eventually leave be feeling drained. This was because I hadn't learnt how to set energetic boundaries for myself, where I would be able to hold my own energy and stop others from infiltrating and intruding on my space. Evidentially, the people I would come into contact with day to day, would rob me of my high positive energy (which I had been working hard to maintain) and leave me with their low negative crappy energy. It is no real wonder I was worn out!

However, I learnt an awful lot from spending a year in a busy city, I finally understood myself to be an empath. Although I was tired most of the time it enabled me to finally learn how to hold my energy better and shield myself from others. It was the only way an empath could survive in a heavily populated place. Many big cities, are almost intrusive of personal space, especially on public transport. It is not energetically healthy for an empath or sensitive person to be in such close proximity to other people. They will easily pick up others energy in these environments unless they can learn to develop strong firm boundaries. If you are in public places often, then start to use these as practice in maintaining energetic boundaries. I would even suggest avoiding rush hours and extremely busy areas if possible, until you have developed firm enough boundaries to be able to handle these places.

How to Set Boundaries

Empaths have the problem of not being able to feel their own needs deeply enough because they are so overwhelmed by the feelings and wants of others. This is why they need to develop even stronger boundaries than a non-empathic person.

Their boundaries are far too permeable to others when they should instead be much firmer in order to provide them with a strong energetic foundation of support. Lacking adequate boundaries in our interactions with others, means we find it extremely difficult to say no, which can often lead to empaths being taken advantage of. One of the hardest things for an empath to understand (because of the way they are made to feel) is that it is not their job to make others happy. They must learn how to make themselves happy first.

The first step in creating healthier boundaries is by increasing your self-confidence. Most of us have been brought up and conditioned through society and by our caregivers that being agreeable means that we are well behaved and therefore good. With these types of beliefs, we often disown our own opinions which results in a lack of confidence. This is a violation against our true selves especially when we carry these types of beliefs into adulthood. Following the exercises in this book will help to improve your self-confidence, there are also countless sources available online for helping increase confidence.

The second step in setting a strong energetic boundary is to be in non-resistance to the other people we are protecting ourselves from. This can be initially quite difficult, especially if others have been infiltrating our space for some time. But without releasing this resistance, we will be unable to prevent them from breaking our boundaries again. It is easy to judge people who are impeding on us. By having an emotional reaction to and judging the people we are trying to keep out, we actually make it easier for them to penetrate our boundary again, which weakens it even further.

The next key to developing boundaries is to have a strong sense of grounding. This is essentially connecting our body to the Earths energy. The whole energetic area (about an arm's length all around you) should be connected to the Earth, not just the area which we cover physically.

1) Oils and Incense

Plant oils and incense sticks have been used for grounding for thousands of years. Herbs such as sage and cedar are still very popular to help cleanse a negative area while bringing positive energy into it. Sage in particular, which gives off a incense-like scent, is often used to clear negativity. Essential oils can also be used for the same purpose.

2) Water

Water could be described as an empaths best friend. It can be used in numerous ways to help with grounding. Taking a quick shower or bath has an incredible effect as it removes and neutralizes the empaths energy. You can even go out in the rain, go swimming, or just go and sit next to water. Adequate daily consumption of water is also highly recommended. Almost any use of water will have a positive grounding effect.

3) Walk barefoot

Probably the most common grounding technique out there and it's easy to do. Simply remove your shoes and walk on the Earth. It can be in your backyard, out in nature, on the beach or anywhere you feel comfortable. By physically feeling the Earth beneath your feet allows you to feel connected while helping to rebalance your emotional state.

Breathing Techniques for Protection

1) Find a quiet peaceful place. Get yourself into a centered and still mindset. Start by paying all of your attention onto your breath. Breathe in through your nose and out through your mouth.

2) When breathing out imagine creating a bubble around you. However far you envision your breath going out, is what defines your own personal space. Usually an arm's length radius is sufficient.

3) This bubble should encompass all around you, if there was someone close behind, you would easily detect their presence since your bubble is sensitive their energy.

4) Your bubble has the ability to expand and contract. For example, you can consciously make it expand when you're public speaking or at a party, or whenever you need to be expressive or seen. On the other hand, whenever you're are in a busy overwhelming environment or do not want to be noticed, you can constrict your bubble and pull it in

towards your body. This helps protect from being intruded upon by others.

5) During this process, you want to begin working with this bubble. As you breathe in, imagine this bubble pulling inward. But, when breathing outward imagine the bubble expanding. Learn to consciously control this boundary through visualization and through your breath.

6) Working consciously with your breath is the most important factor in this exercise. Focus on your breath whenever you feel you need protection from others or from an over stimulating environment.

7) Always visualize your bubble as a strong boundary which protects you easily. See it as clear with no tears or holes in it.

8) If you feel someone has infiltrated your area with their emotions or energy, during the exhale phase, imagine pushing this unwanted energy out and away from your space. By becoming more conscious of your own space, you will easily become aware when this bubble is penetrated against your wish. This can often be through a feeling or emotion.

9) With practice, you will feel and become aware of the presence of this protective bubble. This will enable you to work with and control it much easier.

10) Everyone has an aura or energy space around them but most people do not take responsibility for what they allow to enter this space. Therefore, they often pick up things which do not belong to them. This technique works to protect your own positive energy by preventing others from robbing it from you or exchanging it for their negativity.

There is no right or wrong way to do this, if it feels right to you, it will serve its intended purpose. Feel free to alter parts of this process if you believe it works better.

Practice these boundary techniques as often as possible or until it becomes habitual. Then eventually you will unconsciously control your bubble of protection without even thinking about it. Reaching this point requires some dedication to the practice.

Without learning how to draw energetic boundaries our aura can become too expansive and project outward from us, up to many meters away. If for example, you have a garden full of animals, unless you build a fence around the garden the animals will roam away and you will likely lose most of them. In the same way, we need to build a metaphorical fence around us to contain our energy. If the aura projects too far outwards, let us say at a 5-meter radius all around, then we will pick up whatever is in that area. When out in public, that is potentially a lot of unwanted energy and things which can stick to us.

Without learning to control the aura through a firm boundary, some of our power and vital life energy is lost. But by making a conscious decision to reclaim your energy by pulling it in towards you significantly reduces any losses. The normal resting place for the aura or energy boundary should be close to the body, no more than an arms width radius. This boundary can be consciously expanded through breathwork and visualizing whenever you need to be seen or heard by others. Exercising to constrict and expand your boundary will strengthen your space and allow you more protection from others while also enabling you to be seen.

Healthy boundaries will also help empaths from losing their vital energy through cracks and leaks in the aura. This usually occurs in crowded public places, as our life force can be rapidly sucked away.

Tips for setting boundaries

Empath Meditation

Meditation should be the corner stone of building a healthy and happier life for an empath. It works to reset the mind and body. Sensitives can meditate while imaging themselves engulfed in a white bubble of light which is made of love and protection. Envision this bubble as something which keeps all negativity out. Similar to the grounding technique above, meditate with the aim to keep yourself guarded from unwanted things. The benefits of meditation are incredible, if you aren't meditating at the moment. Here is another good reason to start.

Scan and Check

Another handy tip for sensitives, is to scan their bodies through their attention and awareness before going out anywhere. By working to feel within your own body and checking for emotions or pains before going out, this will allow you to feel what is already there, in other words what is yours. Then when out of the house, you should be able to detect any different emotions or energies which were not present earlier. This is something you likely picked up from someone else.

Mantra

This is a quick and powerful way to create protection if you don't have the time to meditate or ground yourself. It involves creating a mantra for protection but holding a firm belief in its effectiveness is key. Create a mantra for yourself and memorize it so you can use it if and when you need it. An example, of a protection mantra could be something like *'I am encompassed in the light of love and protection. I am protected against any and all negative energies and their effects. Nothing negative can harm or affect me'.*

You can repeat this mantra in your head or silently to yourself if you feel particularly overwhelmed and feel the need for protection. Affirm this statement while keeping your intention within your body scanning for any physical sensations. This will naturally strengthen your energy and aura.

Block or not?

A final word on boundaries, most empaths will eventually learn how to block all external energy coming their way. Although this is a healthy way to tackle the situation for newly learned sensitives, longer-term this may not be the best solution. By blocking all external energies, we are also blocking positive messages coming our way. To live creatively and fully, we need to recognize what is going on around us. When setting the intention of creating a solid boundary it is beneficial to consciously decide to make it permeable to positive energy, only if you feel comfortable doing this. If you're new to setting energetic boundaries, then it would be best to stick with blocking all energies and then with expertise and time understand what you want to let in and what you do not.

Dietary Habits & Lifestyle Changes for Empaths

It is becoming increasingly evident that the foods we eat have a big impact on our psychological and physical state. This is even more relevant to a sensitive person. Firstly, we need to recognize that our physiology is slightly different from others so our bodies need caring for in different ways. By promoting our health and taking extra care, we can begin to better equip ourselves for the day ahead. If for example, you know you have to go to a business meeting and converse with others, this may usually lead to you feeling worn out by the end. But by preempting this event and making the necessary lifestyle choices, you can improve your ability to handle the situation without hitting a low afterwards. These changes will not only help you handle high stress situations, but feel more in control and allow you to return to normality much quicker. It is important to remember that empaths will usually have to develop new lifestyle habits so that they can experience long-term benefits.

Although Empaths and sensitives require more downtime than others to recover and regenerate themselves back to full energy, this shouldn't be confused with shutting oneself away and avoiding life and the world. Through managing your health, you can learn to thrive anywhere.

To begin we will look at some nutrients which empaths should include in their diet or through supplementation. Many of these work directly with the nervous system to help promote stability.

1) Magnesium

This is a very popular mineral which is needed for many bodily functions. It's particularly helpful when feeling stressed. Empaths naturally experience high levels of stress which uses up all of their magnesium reserves, this often causes them to become deficient in this vital mineral. Magnesium works as a relaxant which is important since sensitives carry a lot of muscular tension and stress in their bodies. Magnesium helps release any feelings of anxiety and depression by naturally allowing the body to relax, which also relives tension.

2) B-complex

Every time we are under strain the body uses this compound to help us cope with stress physiologically. B-complex also helps with anxiety, depression and irritability. B-vitamins play a key role in supporting the nervous system, cardiovascular system and are also beneficial in helping us digest food. Try to find a high-quality B-complex multi-vitamin to help make the nervous system more robust to the daily rigors of being an empath.

3) Valerian

This compound is an herbal medicinal plant. It works to reduce hyper sensitivity and irritability by nourishing the nervous system. It is especially effective after a stressful day. Its benefits include reducing anxiety, improving sleep while promoting stress management.

4) Vitamin C

This is popular vitamin can easily be found through eating a healthy diet. It is great for healing, repairing and boosting immune system function. Excess stress is related to sickness and ill health. Sensitives and empaths can use up their vitamin C stores very quickly if they experience high stress levels. What non-empaths may consider a moderate level of stress, can be considered a high-level of stress for some empaths.

5) Rescue medicine/remedy

This is made up of 5 different flower essences and is also known as a 'Flower Remedy'. Rescue remedy functions on the emotional level by helping restore emotional imbalances which can help us cope with various types of sensitive and stressful situations. It is great for helping with focus while reducing anxiety and depression. It is emotionally soothing.

Adrenal Gland Fatigue

The adrenal glands are situated just above the kidneys. The outer part of these glands, the adrenal cortex, is responsible for producing important hormones such as cortisol and others, these vital hormones work to help the body respond to stress while regulating our metabolism. Cortisol is most popularly known as the stress hormone which is secreted in abundance in response to any fearful situations, also known as the fight of flight response.

When an empath feels worn out and exhausted they can often suffer from adrenal fatigue. This occurs when the adrenal glands natural hormones (which help keep us upbeat and energized), become depleted through stress, anxiety, exhaustion and insomnia. All of these symptoms are very common in empaths, therefore so is adrenal fatigue.

By learning to manage adrenal fatigue we can begin to reverse these symptoms and gradually get a better handle on external stressors. Here are a few things you can do to help –

- Stay away from refined sugars and stimulants - These kick an already sensitive system into overdrive and causes the adrenals to work harder which leads to burnout. Try some fruit instead.
- Exercise - Regular exercise will help to cleanse and clear out your body and adrenals while also helping release any negative emotions you might have picked up.
- Sunlight and fresh air - Try to get out of a stuffy house or office and take in the fresh air and vitamin D from the sun. Both will help heal the adrenals.

Recharging Strategies

Now we will look at some general strategies which will help keep your energy clear and vibrant most of the time. By taking the time to work these practices into your daily life, you'll see a noticeable improvement in your overall health and well-being.

We have a natural ability to positively impact the world but our energy needs to vibrant and clear in order to be truly effective.

Sleep –

Probably the number one regenerative thing an empath can do is to get a good night's sleep, as often as possible. Due to their natural sensitivity, sleep is something we can often struggle with. I personally have certain requirements when it comes to sleeping well. First and foremost, the room must be pitch black with no visible light, secondly, I require it to be deadly silent so you cannot hear a pin drop and finally I need my own bed. Hotels or friends' houses are usually a struggle for me to sleep in. Pay attention to your own sleeping habits and what prerequisites you require.

Empaths need regular deep sleep to help regenerate back to full health. Through this they're able to recharge their sensitive system. If you struggle with sleep, try meditating just before going to bed. Stay away from any medication and sleeping pills as they create long-term sleeping issues due to reliance.

If you're like me, your phone is usually the last thing you look at before going to sleep and the first thing you check in the morning. This could actually be hindering your ability to get a good night's sleep. Research has suggested that the light given off by our electronic gadgets such as phones and tablets hinders the adequate release of the hormone melatonin, this is an important hormone in the regulation of healthy sleep patterns. The less you release the harder it will be to fall asleep. Again, the light of these electronics will most likely impact empaths and sensitives more. So, try switching these devices off at least one hour before you hit the sack.

I have personally found listening to a relaxing audiobook or some meditation music helps me to nod off naturally. Try to get to sleep by 10pm if possible. The human body functions just like the natural cycles of mother nature. Sleeping my 10pm optimizes our hormones and important chemicals which determine our energy levels, how we feel and our vitality. If we are out of synch with this cycle, we will pay the price.

Sleep deprivation for an empath can be very distressing. The importance of a good night's sleep cannot be overstated.

Sea Salt Bath -

When feeling overwhelmed or stressed, take the time to have a bath. Grab a few handfuls of sea salt and add it to your bath. The added salt will work to cleanse and revitalize your energy field by washing away any negative energy. Before getting in send an intention to the bath water, to cleanse you completely. Soak in the bath for at least half an hour.

Smoothies -

Eating and following a healthy lifestyle is very important for sensitives as we react badly to the additives and artificial ingredients added to a lot of food these day. A great healthy and tasty way to get more goodness into your diet is through daily smoothies. Simply go and buy some green vegetables and fruits, throw them all together into a juicer or blender to make a nutritious delicious smoothie. The color of your smoothie can resonate with the body's chakras. The color green, for example, resonates with the heart chakra, which is our central chakra. Empowering this chakra will create clarity into your aura and energy field. You can effectively make smoothies of any color, to help empower your body's natural intelligence.

Many resources are available for various recipes to help make the most nutritious shakes. Find the ones which suit you best!

Stimulants such as caffeine are over-stimulating for empaths. This external source of energy is so easily absorbed by sensitives that it can cause mental confusion. For most of my life, I felt I had an attention disorder as I was unable to hold my attention for long periods of time, it was only through realizing that I was incredibly sensitive to the food I was eating that I was able to clean up my diet. This allowed be get a handle on this mental short-coming and overtime gradually increase my ability to concentrate.

Empaths and sensitives, can sometimes struggle to be present with a high degree of focused concentration since they're easily distracted or stimulated by some external stimulus they pick up on. This makes it difficult to function at their best particularly in public places where they're surrounded by many people, such as schools or workplaces.

Being an empath requires a lot of close introspection through really understanding our bodies and how what we put into them impacts how we feel. Creating a journal is a great way to start to understand yourself and what works for you.

Practical exercises for Empaths

Shutting yourself from others is incredibly harmful psychologically for anyone, not just for empaths. This increases the sensitivity we feel when around others. We want to be able to function at our best in all situations and not become overly sensitive to 'regular' people.

A method many sensitives use unconsciously to stop the constant bombardment of others emotions and energy, is to distract themselves. Distracting works to lessen the impact of external stimulus. But there are various negative forms of distraction such as alcohol, drugs, sex, porn and junk food which can lead to a reliance or an unhealthy addiction. Most of these addictions shift our perception into a state where we are not as aware, this allows us to escape feeling the pain in the world. Try to avoid these at all costs!

In this chapter, we will look at positive exercises and forms of distraction which will help support you no matter what you're faced with without relying on unhealthy vices.

Using Affirmations

Many people use affirmations nowadays, they have become incredibly popular in all walks of life. They're positive statements repeated over and over to help us escape negative thought patterns while promoting positive ones. They can help keep an empath strong particularly in an overwhelming situation. You can create your own affirmations if something in particular resonates with you. Here are a few of the ones which I have found helpful -

'I refuse to absorb other people's energy. I can acknowledge how others are feeling, but I now shield myself from absorbing anything from them'.

'I can allow others close to me, without taking on their energy or emotions'.

'I feel and connect with my own feelings before anyone else's'.

Assertiveness tip –

Do you struggle saying no to people? This is a common occurrence among sensitives, here is an idea which I found helpful when presented with something I wasn't sure about. If for example, a friend of colleague asks you out for drinks in the evening, instead of agreeing immediately, respond with 'Ok, I will just have to check my schedule and let you know' - This isn't saying no! But it is in fact giving you some breathing space to decide whether or not this is something you want to do. With this kind of response, you don't feel like you have been put on the spot and that you must respond immediately. This gives you time to process the request and hopefully muster up the courage within to say no (if you don't feel like doing what was requested). Beginning to honor your feelings is incredibly important.

Here are three unfinished sentences which you can work with to help build your sense of boundaries. Try to come up with as many different responses as you can. By doing this you are gradually beginning to reinforce and develop stronger boundaries.

1) I have the right to ask for.........

Some answer here could include - space, respect etc.

2) To have enough time and energy to function at my best, it is ok to..........

Examples - refuse invitations, do my own work first etc.

3) If I refuse others, they may......

Examples - not like me, talk badly about me, respect me more etc

Without talking care of your own boundaries, you are effectively hindering yourself from living a happy and successful life. That's what it comes down to. Over time, this becomes easier. Helping others at your own expenses is detrimental to the whole.

Exercise

Exercise is an absolute must. I have personally found it to be one of the main tools I use that helps me enjoy life as an empath. The right training will not only exercise the physical body but the nervous system also (the root of your sensitivity). By exercising to engage the nervous system, we can almost reset our minds and bodies. This is exactly how I feel after a workout, as though someone has pushed a button and I have been energetically reset. It works incredibly well to clear away negative or any stagnant energy. It also increases the flow of freshly oxygenated blood all around the body. These are just some of the many benefits associated to exercise.

Another important tip is to stay away from public mirrors. The ones you find in gyms and clothes shops. Empaths can pick up negative energies being reflected to them from mirrors especially if the people who have been looking at their reflections are egotistical or self-absorbed. The empath can often take on this negative energy as their own.

Clearing your energy to create healthier boundaries

Reduce negativity - Due to our sensitive nature, we pick up negativity very easily. To help overcome this, empaths should start distancing themselves from negativity as much as possible. This can include people you know, certain places, even the news and social platforms. The TV and social media can really impact the empath on a subconscious level, they may not realize it at the time but they are picking up a lot of negativity from these sources particularly from the news, world affairs, soap operas and even reality TV shows.

Balance - Living a balanced life, is important for anyone, none more so than for an empath. This includes all areas of life such as diet, work, health, sleep, exercise etc. Keeping all aspects in some kind of balance help help avoid becoming over stimulated. Try not to overdo it, as you'll likely need longer to recover. I have personally found I can only exercise 2-3 times a week, any more than this and I tend to feel burnt out. Taking adequate rest is also important and will improve your overall health and well-being.

Determine what is not yours –

Sometimes we walk into a room or a situation and feel like we have energetically picked up a mood or a vibe which wasn't ours. Try to bring your conscious awareness to any feelings you suspect don't belong to you. If you don't feel it is yours then make a choice to discard it, send the unwanted energy away and down into the earth. This can be done easily, simply holding your focus and stating the intention in your mind while visualizing the emotion leaving you.

Declutter –

Since empaths fundamentally must claim ownership over their own energetic space and stop others intruding in it, they should also take the same care with their physical areas. If you are messy, untidy or have a lot of clutter, take the time to clear your physical space, doing this will clear your mind and energy also. Negativity tends to breed in clutter and mess.

Crystals for protection –

Crystals are a gift and a spiritual super power for promoting self-care. Anything can be used as a symbol of protection whether that is a piece of jewelry or a crystal. The most important thing is that you believe in whatever you are trusting for your protection. This belief alone will help protect you. People find it easy to trust in crystals due to their natural Earthly healing properties and they're fairly inexpensive to buy. If you are interested in learning in depth knowledge on how to use crystals and how to get the most out of these powerful stones then please check out my other book - Crystal Healing: Heal Yourself & Transform Your Life.

Now we will take a look at some crystals which work incredibly well as protection for empaths and sensitives.

Rose Quartz

This is a great crystal for empaths to possess simply for its grounding properties. It is often referred to as the 'Love Stone', since is resonates and works to repair the heart chakra. These qualities give the user a boost while helping to keep others negative emotions out of their space. It promotes all types of love, such as self-love, romantic, unconditional and platonic. Since it is a quartz, this means it has a high energy that can help bring a positive loving vibration into almost all circumstances. By bringing more love into an empaths daily life, it helps to lower stress while carrying warmth to everyone who is present. It is also used to improve self-esteem and attract genuine love into our lives. All these positive qualities bring balance to the emotions while helping to reduce stress and anxieties.

Black Tourmaline

This has been referred to as the 'must have' crystal for empaths. Known for its protective qualities this crystal enables the carrier to shield and deflect away any negative or low vibrational energies. It does this by processing any bad energy which comes into the auric field whether it's from other people or the environment. It also acts as a filter to protect us, which only allows good energies in, such as love, joy and kindness.

When carried regularly it neutralizes and purifies our own negative thought patterns by filtering them into positive energy. It is renowned as an extremely effective grounding stone, it achieves this by creating a connection between the body and Earth. This contact helps to align and balance the energy centers (chakras) while channeling positive healing energy through the whole physical body.

Sugilite

This crystal comes in a striking violet color and resonates with the 7th chakra - the crown. It creates a firm impermeable bubble around the carrier which helps protect them from negative energies of the environment and unwanted thought forms from others. It's incredibly effective at preventing energetic attacks from energy vampires by dissolving the bad energy patterns headed our way. Its power enables the user to go through their daily activities with a sense of inner strength and grace. Due to its activation of the crown chakra, it helps bring healing light in from the head down to the 1st chakra - the root. This influx of positive energy promotes balance and well-being that keeps us strong when faced with negativity.

Lapis Lazuli

A very popular and attractive stone that has been used for many thousands of years, particularly prevalent with the ancient Egyptians. It is best known for its protective qualities and its ability to repair, seal and strengthen the auric field. This helps in dissolving any negative emotions or energies which have been picked up. Lapis is a crystal of truth which helps increase self-awareness within the empath, with this we become more conscious of what belongs to us and what doesn't. In the same way, it allows what doesn't belong to us to be released and 'brought to the surface'. Lapis works with the third eye chakra, which is the seat of perception, with this we are able to gain clarity and 'see' exactly what is occurring around us energetically. Although, empaths sense this, they do not always clearly understand what is happening. It also helps promote grounding and restores balance.

Breathing Techniques

The 4-7-8 method

Every empath should possess at least one breathing technique in their tool box, the most popular one I use it called the 4-7-8 breathing method. This comes from Yoga and is often used to help reduce anxiety.

1) Place the tip of the tongue onto the roof of your mouth, right behind the top front teeth. This allows the muscles in your face to relax. You must keep your tongue in this position for the whole exercise. The technique can be performed in any position, standing, lying or sitting down. If used while sitting down, ensure the feet are planted firmly on the ground while sitting up straight.

2) Once in a suitable position. Breathe out all the air in your lungs out through the mouth.

3) Next, close the mouth, and begin to inhale deeply through the nostrils while mentally counting to 4.

4) Hold the breath for a count of 7.

5) Exhale the breath out from the mouth while counting to 8.

6) Repeat this breath cycle for 4 times. This shouldn't take much longer than 30 seconds.

This quick technique naturally alters our state into a more pleasant consciousness. It promotes a sense of relaxation especially when practiced a few times a day. For sensitives who struggle to sleep, this method can help relax you into sleep very quickly. It can also help reduce the fear response of fight or flight within the body, which naturally reduces anxiety and any stress related hormones.

Releasing Negative Emotions –

Empaths and sensitives are naturally emotional and therefore they're more susceptible to crying. This isn't necessarily a bad thing however, as this tendency can be used to help clear out negative emotions. When we work on ourselves through studying, reading, meditations, therapy or by whatever means, the old unwanted energies need to detach and be released from our physical bodies. These old energetic patterns can be let go off through crying, this is a healthy way to release. I am not suggesting crying all day and night, but letting the tears out once in a while, will do more good, than keeping them locked in. You can even try to invoke crying by watching a sad movie or listening to a song which you find deeply moving, this will usually trigger the release of any unwanted energetic pain. Crying is a natural human process and something which should be seen as necessary and healthy. We have been lead to believe that crying is a weakness when in fact it is a sign of strength which will only make us stronger and more emotionally robust. During a bout of crying, feel as though you're letting go of old unwanted things and see yourself growing into something greater. This makes the very act of crying a positive empowering ritual.

Use crowded places

As we know, empaths and sensitives don't like being out in public places for too long. This problem can be approached in a different way however. We can use busy places as practice in developing our boundaries. When in a packed area, envision your boundaries constricting inward around you and completely shielding you from all negative external energies. We are effectively using public places as a training ground for learning to set boundaries. This is much more effective than practicing setting boundaries when you're alone at home.

Also, by going out with someone you are energetically compatible with (family member, partner or friend), acts as a further defense to your boundary. Both you and the other persons' energy will create a stronger shield around both of you. Further helping to distract and dispel any unwanted energies. You may have noticed that you do not feel as drained when out with a friend in public. This also works to distract you from external stimulus, as your focus is naturally more on the person whom you are with.

Yoga Poses

Yoga is ancient art form which has been used for many years to help empower people. We can use it in helping to create stronger boundaries around ourselves. The best poses for empaths are generally the ones which allow us to open up the body and reclaim our space. By holding these positions and breathing deeply into them before going out, strengthens our energetic space and aura.

Some of the best poses for this include, the star fish pose, this involves standing up straight with your legs and arms spread out wide. The other popular pose is called the warrior pose. Both of these poses make you take up space with your body, the space you take up is your energetic area. By doing these poses before heading out, you are setting your boundaries and stopping anything unwanted coming in. By expanding your aura and energy field in this way, you may become more noticeable, but you will feel much safer also.

Warrior Pose

Music/Audio

Listening to music through headphones while out can be greatly beneficial to help distract from the constant barrage of stimulus around you, providing you have done the work of setting a firm energetic boundary prior. Listening to audio can be extremely effective because it directs your focus inward to what you're listening to. I have personally found audiobooks the most beneficial as I can concentrate on what is being said. With music, I sometimes tend to switch off. Although both are effective, find what works best for you. Audio helps to further strengthen your boundaries since only you can hear what's coming through the headphones, this automatically removes you from the energetic flow of everyone else and reinforces the protective bubble around you.

Comfort Zone

I believe that working with our comfort zone is one of the keys to long-term growth for empaths or anyone else, for that matter. Learning to push ourselves past what we feel comfortable with helps build inner strength. We can be sensitive and strong! Empaths often struggle to move out of their comfort zones for the simple fact it is more uncomfortable for them to do so, compared to non-empaths. No matter what the situation is, whether it is going out into public places, or speaking out when you would usually stay quiet, you must learn to go inward and muster up the strength to face challenges head-on. I wish I could tell you there was a short cut and that being an empath was all plain sailing but if you truly want to find real fulfillment in life you must step out of your comfort zone. Firstly, with small steps and then gradually build up as you gain momentum. All empaths have something they would like to do or achieve but have often allowed their sensitivity to hold them back. The only way through this resistance is through it. If there is something you have always dreamed about, I urge you to make this a future goal and with focused action and courage, trust that you will eventually reach this destination. It won't be easy but it will certainly be worth it. The confidence and belief this builds within, is unspeakable.

Healing Yourself

We often hear about empaths abilities to help and heal others. But to maximize this talent we need to be fully healed first. Thankfully, we not only have the intuitive ability to heal others but also any emotional wound or disease within ourselves also. How powerful of a healer you become depends on your intention, belief, imagination while living with an open loving heart and mind.

Many empaths wounds come from a lack of self-esteem and trust. Not just trust in others, but a lack of trust in themselves. They may have experienced hurt through a close loved one, which has created these wounds within them. If you are able to pin point which experience caused your biggest emotional wounds than that is a great place to start. If you're not sure, then trust your instincts, they will guide you in the right direction.

Rebuilding low self-esteem can be particularly difficult for empaths, especially as they put others needs ahead of their own. Beginning to realize that they do not need to sacrifice their own happiness for anyone else's is an important realization. You matter, your feelings matter just as much as the next persons. You may have felt that caring for others meant you should neglect your own needs so you could help those who need you. But with this type of behavior, your kindness will often be taken as a weakness, which will cause others to walk all over you. Healthy relationships are based upon reciprocity, which involves giving and taking in equal amounts.

When viewing all your relationships, begin to give more attention to those people who acknowledge you and hold a healthy degree of self-love for themselves. This means staying away from narcissistic types and energy vampires. Once you make the intention to put yourself first, you naturally start withdrawing your energy from unhealthy relationships. You instead direct that energy into yourself and with those who are genuine and caring individuals. This helps to significantly decrease stress and any anxiety related to your personal relationships.

Returning another's energy

In this exercise, we will set the intention to send the others negative energy or emotion back to where it came from. First acknowledge if you feel any trauma, pain or negative energy that is weighing down on you. Try not to judge the person this has come from. Realize, that by taking on this person's feelings or emotions, you're not helping them. They need to experience their own emotions and learn to grow through them by overcoming their own pain. When taking on others emotions, we are effectively preventing them from growing and developing. You can simply return the energy to the sender by clearing your auric/energy field or set the intention and visualize sending these feeling back to them. Use your imagination, these feelings can take any shape or form which looks appropriate to you. The intention is the most important part of this exercise.

Psychotherapy

Talking therapy with a qualified practitioner is one of the most popular ways of emotional healing. It involves discussing any psychological disorders or emotional problems that we are experiencing with a registered professional. It works by allowing the patient to freely discuss and talk about their feelings, in order to gain a greater understanding of themselves, which leads to greater healing, relief from their problems and increased self-confidence.

It is especially effective for empaths, as it gives them a safe space to be heard where they won't be judged. Combining talking therapy with other healing modalities such as EFT (emotional freedom techniques), somatic therapy and breathwork can help amplify therapy's effectiveness. Using these various techniques together allows negative residual energies and trauma which has been stored in the body to finally be released. Empaths will take on and store a lot of trauma, from others as well as their own. By processing this through the mentioned methods, you can finally begin to let it go and put it all behind you. With this freedom from the past comes a brand-new enthusiasm for the future and a life you can truly enjoy. Healing begins to correct and reprogram limiting beliefs and any dysfunctional thought patterns.

Protection Against Energy Vampires and Psychic Attacks

'Energy vampires are emotionally immature individuals who have the sense that the whole world revolves around them. They are almost incapable of seeing things from another person's perspective. They often lack empathy' – PsychCentral (3)

Most sensitives have been around or come across energy vampires or narcissistic people at some point. Even after spending a few minutes in their company we often leave feeling violated and drained. In my experience, most emotional vampires are not aware of this trait within them but that doesn't help us not feel terrible in their company. Even though they may be oblivious to their own nature, most of them unconsciously recognize that being around an empath makes them feel better and more positive about themselves. For this reason, they can often cling to empaths because of the positive feelings they are able to gain from being in their presence. Due to an energy vampires overbearing personality, empaths often struggle against these types of energetic attacks because of their weak boundaries. Being around them can negatively impact their own ability to function well. After spending too much time with these people, our energy begins to diminish into negativity, whereas the energy vampire feels uplifted from taking positive energy from us. They essentially feed on others positivity. It is important to recognize if you feel depleted, stressed or drained around certain people as you're likely in the presence of a psychic vampire.

The Reasons Behind Vampirism & Narcissism

These people feel cut off from themselves and deep down feel unworthy of being loved which stops them from getting their own needs met. The only way they can get what they need is to take it from others. Due to their unconnectedness to themselves they are unable to find fulfillment within, so this void is then filled by stealing energy from other people. They prey on easy targets, i.e. those with weak boundaries who can easily to drained.

Energy vampires are often singled out for being evil and harmful but their actions are often unconscious. They don't know what they are doing. They are victims themselves, although this doesn't make it any easier on us. The paradox is that the energy vampire and the victim are similar on some level. They have been drawn together and that is why the vampire is able to attach to the victim through this identification. The opposites have attracted one another.

Narcissists are often attracted to empaths and people in healing or spiritual circles as these people are the most open and loving. This makes them easy prey for an energy vampire. They will usually stay attached to these people for a long time, due to the victim's non-resistance. On the surface it will probably look like a positive friendship.

It is also worth mentioning that while certain people are energy vampires per se, most people have some vampirism tendencies depending upon their mood. If someone you know, a friend perhaps, is going through a particularly tough time they may unconsciously reach out in an energy sucking way, as they seek an uplift in their mood. They probably won't realize they are doing this but empaths should be on their guard against it. Telephone calls are one of the main ways friends can steal your energy. If a friend calls you regularly to talk about their problems, you may want to emotionally withdraw and detach consciously from the conversation. Be there to listen but not to take on their negative energy. Over time your friend will probably recognize they do not get a boost from unloading their problems onto you, so will probably stop sharing their personal issues as much. This doesn't mean your friendship with them will end but you are just setting a boundary between what is yours and what is theirs. Remember that healthy relationships are based on balance and an equal amount of giving and taking.

Energetic Cording

The primary way I have found to disconnect from these people is to cut them out of my life and stop communicating with them altogether. Not in a malicious way, but instead to essentially release them through love and forgiveness. This can be incredibly difficult to do however, especially if it is someone close such as a family member or a work colleague we have to see each day. In these scenarios, we can disconnect from the other by cutting our energetic ties to them.

'Cording' refers to an energetic connection between two people. These connections are usually between certain chakras. For example, when a mother gives birth to a baby they're energetically connected via the first charka (at the bottom of the torso). The root chakra from the mother connects to the root chakra to the baby. It would essentially look like a line of light from one to the other, this a healthy positive cord.

Healthy energetic cords can also form between people who are not related, such as spouses, close friends or anyone you feel a connection too. However, these cord connections can also be forced by one person onto another. This type of cording is unhealthy and draining to the recipient of such an act.

For example, people often become attached to their ex-partners. Even after the relationship is over, we can sometimes still feel a connection to this person. It is possible that your ex-partner had created a cord into your system to remember and to stay in touch with you energetically. This enables them to experience a little bit of your energy. When your ex is thinking or remembering you, they are creating and reinforcing an energetic cord into one of your chakras, probably unconsciously. This is why, even after the relationship is over, we cannot stop thinking about the other person. They are connecting to us energetically. That's why it is important to heal your own energy to stop other people cording into you again.

Most energetic cording takes place on one of the torso based charkas (1 to 4) these include the sacral (above the groin area), the solar plexus (mid-belly), the heart or the throat chakra. If you feel an ache or sensation in any of these areas when around a certain person, become aware that they may be draining your life force from you. You can block this by simply placing your hands directly over the affected chakra to help break the connection. Often in difficult social situations, people will cross their arms over their bodies (usually unconsciously), this helps us feel safer and defend our energy in this position.

The reason another person is able to cord you is because your chakras are not strong enough and must be healed. When the chakras are unhealthy or unhealed it leaves them open for others to attach to. Psychic vampires gain a strong feed of energy from the chakra points. For example, a person I used to know would attach to my solar plexus and I could physically feel the sensation of the connection. When the chakras and boundaries are healed, healthy and established, it becomes difficult for others to form this connection though cording your energy field. Energetic cords form when we still carry hurt or baggage with us from our pasts. These wounds leave our chakras open so they become easily attachable. The low energy of this wound attracts the low energy of the vampire or narcissist.

Empaths often feel a sensation in their solar plexus region. This chakra is the seat of our emotions. This is where the emotions of others are most deeply felt and where we are the most vulnerable to be corded and drained. Weakness in this area can cause digestive system and stomach problems.

Cord Cutting Exercise

Toxic draining relationships require what is often referred to as cord cutting. Once energetic cords are established it can be difficult to break them without conscious intention. If you feel drained from certain family members, ex-partners, work colleagues or anyone whom you have close regular contact with then it may be time to repair your connection to them. You might sense that this other person sends you negative, harmful thoughts and energy, even when you're not close to them.

If you feel you have been corded then this cord cutting exercise will help release it.

1) Imagine the other person and envision a cord or tube connecting the two of you, from one of your chakras.

2) Next visualize a cutting tool (such as scissors or sword) slicing through and cutting the cord at your chakra point.

3) Ask for the other person's energy to be returned to them and yours to be returned to you. Visualize this in your mind.

4) Following this, ask yourself what negative belief you were holding which attracted this experience to you in the first place? With this realization, we begin to see that we are not innocent helpless victims but in fact we are attracting these experiences to us, for a chance to overcome and grow through them.

5) Realize your self-worth as an empath is not dependent on helping others. This is a common misconception which leads to us attracting the wrong relationships.

6) End the exercise by forgiving the other party and releasing them with love.

Meditation

If you have left an interaction with an energy vampire and feel drained, this is a great time to clear the connection. This can also be achieved through meditation.

1) Close your eyes and begin by making yourself comfortable.

2) Scan your body from the head down to the feet and pay attention to any attachments you feel. It shouldn't be too difficult to determine what part of the body you are being drained from.

3) Upon determining what part of the body you feel this connection too, look to see the shape or form of the connection. See a physical representation of this energetic attachment. To me, it looks like an energetic tube which sucks energy in.

4) Begin cutting the attachment away from you. Envision you have a sword made of light and see this sword cutting through these attachments which are then being released from your body.

5) Once the attachment or cord is removed. You must apply healing to the area by placing your hand over the chakra and send healing energy to the area. See the open chakra begin to restore. Allow it to heal and repair itself.

6) As the chakra is healed visualize a new vibrancy and boost of energy within it.

7) Send the other person's energy and attachment back to them. There is no harm in this, it was their stuff in the first place.

8) Scan your whole body again noticing if there are any other attachments or sensations. If you do sense something carry out the same detaching for the new area.

9) Finally, envision a white light surrounding and protecting you. This bubble of protection will always remain with you unless you decide to release it.

You can practice this meditation almost anywhere. At work, on public transport or anywhere you are able to go within for a few moments.

The key to dealing with psychic attacks from unhealthy people is simply becoming more aware. Often energy vampires appear friendly, attractive and charismatic, which draws us in. The fact that they show us attention usually allows us to let them close to us. It is not our responsibility to heal these people. At least, not until we have healed ourselves first.

Embracing Your Gift

This 'gift' is often seen as a curse and much of this book has focused on many of the negative traits of empaths. But this was important to help you learn how to manage and understand yourself better, so you can step into this gift and use it to its fullest capacity. Many of the so called 'negative' traits are actually the positive ones as well, they're just viewed in a different light. It's like double-edged sword, with which we're looking to effectively negate the negative effects by transmuting them into positive benefits.

Empaths have had feelings of over sensitivity since birth. So from day one, their brains have been wired up through neural connections to compensate for their natural alertness and sensitivity. Neural pathways are connections all brains make through repeated action. The more we do something, the stronger the associated neural pathways become established within the mind and through repetition these actions eventually become a habit. For example, if you avoided eye contact with others from a young age because you felt a powerful hit of their emotions, your brain will have created the connections to avoid eye contact each time you come into contact with someone, until eventually it became an unconscious habit.

For this reason, many of the behaviors expressed by empaths are deeply ingrained within their psyche via years of repetition through defending themselves. It can be incredibly difficult to change these deep-seated behaviors and beliefs. The easiest way around this is to build upon the tendencies which are already present. Building upon established neural pathways with new connections will be the easiest way to reinforce new behaviors.

The first step is to fully own and accept this trait as a gift. It is the only way we can begin to harness the power it holds. For many years, I used to hate this trait. I did whatever I could to try and overcome it, wrongfully thinking that it was a psychological programming that I had picked up from my mother. But in fact, it was my mother's genetic predisposition towards sensitivity which had been passed down to me. I then realized I was stuck with it, through this I learnt to accept it as part of myself and how to work with it.

Fighting against it lead to some difficult challenges in my life from my earliest years. I was incredibly shy growing up, I was very sensitive to pain and easily distracted which lead to anxiety in my adult life. It was only through owning this part of myself that I was able to begin functioning at a higher level. Learning how to protect myself, allowed me to find more happiness. This is what I want for you. I know how difficult it can be being an empath, we often feel so different, so misunderstood, left out and not part of normal society. But, as I learnt, we are special.

You can start to understand these gifts more, by beginning to pay closer attention to yourself through non-judgement and non-resistance. For instance, I have had always an expansive aura which I hated, as I would always be noticed by others which was terrible for me since I was incredibly shy. I saw this as a negative part of myself. But as I learnt to work with this gift, I understood that I could affect the energy of an entire room with my presence. People would tell me I was kind and would be grateful for my attention. They would tell me deeply personal things, from only having met them for a few minutes. Sometimes they would even comment, 'why am I telling you this? I barely even know you'. Of course, I knew why they were opening their heart to me, it was because I was truly hearing what they had to say.

This is a gift which should be used through your own conscious decision. You decide if you want someone to unload their issues onto you. This is only achieved through setting boundaries. By doing this, I built my self-confidence up and started to trust myself more. Animals loved me. I discovered I was very visually creative, that I enjoyed writing and that I could communicate with others in a way which I had never known. I still continue to find out new things about myself all of the time, it's great! I genuinely believe the same is possible for each and every empath out there.

Your talents

The ability to connect with others better, to really put yourself into their shoes and understand where they are coming from is a trait of immeasurable value. This can be used in any number of professions from sales, to medicine to therapy. People with this skill will never struggle to find work. The world needs more genuinely caring and understanding people.

Empaths have a high degree of introspection. With their sensitivity, they can direct this power inward, towards themselves. This helps make them very intuitive, providing they can quieten their minds from any mental chatter. Learning to work and trust this intuition over time, will begin to guide your life in the right direction.

This sixth sense will make it easier to connect and discover your true calling in life, your deepest purpose. This can be a struggle for many people, but empaths usually have an in-built knowing about what they are capable of achieving and where their true passions lie. They may often need to develop the courage to go after their dreams but finding what they are here to do isn't usually a problem.

Healing

This is the natural ability to heal ourselves and others. To truly achieve this skill, we need to have developed and learnt to separate our emotions from others. Putting ourselves into another person's shoes while seeing and feeling what they experience is a treasure to behold. But it can be a difficult to handle. Being able to understand others in this way allows us to treat them with more compassion. By picking up on their history and their hurt we are able to become powerful transformative healers.

Empaths are naturally drawn to professions which involve healing others, they can have great careers as therapists and in alternative healing methods such as Reiki practitioners, hypnotherapists and such.

They can also heal through feeling another's emotions. By getting in tune with another's pain, they help heal the patient through a combined transmutation of their emotional trauma. Connecting to the pain in another person, allows the skilled empath to draw this pain out of them (with the intention of the patient).

They can even help uncover hidden emotional issues through sensing others emotional blocks, then helping the person to begin working through them. In this way, they provide great guidance and help for directing inner healing. This skill is most effective if someone is stuck on a particular issue and requires guidance on how to move forward.

Telepathy/Psychic -

It is generally believed that everyone has a certain degree of psychic ability, which allows us to see into past or future events with which we have no connection too. This is usually done unconsciously, with little intention. But, when it happens, it usually leaves us in awe and shock. Unsurprisingly, since empaths are attuned to picking up on subtleties in energy, they also possess a natural talent for telepathy. They can correctly predict future events through a hunch which is referred to as precognition.

Empaths can function on various levels of psychic work, these can include Mediumship which involves working with and sensing spirits. Many also have a natural ability to connect with and understand animals on a deeper level, so professions which require working with animals can give them a lot of satisfaction.

Some use their abilities through a skill called Geomancy, this is where they have honed their abilities to feel the energies of the Earth. With this sense, they can order, detect and predict water flow and the weather.

It can be frustrating trying to understand why we have this ability while looking to uncover our life's purpose. But by using your natural talents, abilities and interests as a guide, they will help take you to your truth.

Help Raise the Vibrational frequency of the Planet

Just by our sheer presence on earth we help transmute negative energies, without even knowing we are. This alone makes us indispensable. Empaths mop up the crap created by others, especially in times of huge negativity. Increasing the vibration of the planet is essentially Gods work or at least a highly spiritual undertaking.

We can increase our ability to do this through self-love and caring for ourselves first. By nurturing all of our health we promote our natural talents and then by following our interests, the path ahead begins clear, this adds positive vibrations to the planet. If whatever you do is from a place of love, you will always find happiness.

You'll notice a big shift when you start to look towards thriving in this world, instead of just being in survival mode (which is what most of us have been used to). Being brave enough to take the steps in the direction of your goals and dreams, is when the real magic begins to happen. So instead of always seeing your gifts as a hindrance, start to move into their true power.

I personally believe empaths have a great strength because of what they have already had to endure through life, the pain and the hurt. This strength which has built up should be harnessed and used to propel you forwards to conquer new heights while positively impacting the planet.

6th sense

Empaths view of the world through their sensing emotions, feelings and energies effectively creates within them a 6th sense. If it was taken away from us, we would most probably be left feeling stuck. We would lose so much of what this gift gives us and what we also take for granted, as we predominately focus on its negative aspects. Being able to tell when someone is lying or telling the truth or being able to sense others pain and if they need healing are all forms of guidance.

Sometimes our help will be dismissed which can be upsetting especially when we see another person hurting. But some people need to experience their suffering to allow them to grow and awaken so they can create a better life for themselves. It is their journey. If there was no resistance, there would be nothing to force us to grow stronger. Difficult circumstances can sometimes be seen as an insurmountable mountain, but they must be tackled head on. Overcoming these challenges might be painful and difficult, but the view from the top of the mountain along with the inner gold you will discover, makes it all worthwhile.

Conclusion

Congratulations! I am incredibly proud of you for making it to the end of this book. It truly lets me know that there are people are out there who are genuinely interested in reaching their fullest potential, this is something the world needs more of. I am convinced that if each and every empath on our planet learnt more about how to harness this special gift and bring it out, then the world we live in would look very different. We are needed here and have great work to do, with that comes a great responsibility and we can only take this on by first taking care of ourselves. Once we know how to do this, only then can we extend and reach out to help others on their journey.

It is important to remember that everyone's experience of life is different. So it is important you begin to look within yourself for more answers and recognize that the keys to change begin with you. Look at your life as a fun journey of self-exploration. If someone were to ask me now, if I would change my empathic nature, the simple answer would be no. I have learnt to work with and embrace all the gifts it has given me, without this ability I wouldn't be me.

I hope by using the knowledge in this book you're able to find more joy and fulfillment in your daily life. Everyone deserves to be happy but for some of us this can be more challenging. Stepping into your power and making a commitment to improve your life, is the single most important thing in creating change. So look within for your courage. If there is one thing I have learnt from being an empath, that is that we are incredibly strong and can endure a lot. It is about time we started to direct this strength towards creating a happier and more joyful life for ourselves.

Once you learn to work with this gift, you will experience more incredible moments than you have ever known. A fully engaged empath, who knows how to manage their gift, can be so fully absorbed in reality that every moment becomes pure joy. Reaching this level takes dedication and work but with practice you'll experience the bliss of living a full life. Feeling every moment is the key to real joy and happiness.

Thank you!

Resources

1) Social cognition in social anxiety: first evidence for increased empathic abilities. Tibi-Elhanany Y[1], Shamay-Tsoory SG. (2011)

2) http://www.briantracy.com

3) https://psychcentral.com/blog/.../11/.../how-to-avoid-being-drained-by-energy-vampires

4) http://naturalfamilytoday.com/health/6-effective-grounding-techniques-for-empaths/

Empath –

A Spiritual and Emotional Healing Guide to Personal Transformation for Highly Sensitive People (Vol.2)

by

Marianne Gracie

Introduction

The world needs empaths. They have the ability to raise the vibration of not only their immediate environment, but collectively of the whole planet. You may have experienced that when you're around you seem to increase the harmony within a group. Or that your presence has a soothing and healing effect on others. Imagine if the whole world could simultaneously feel this? It would change everything!

Empaths are only at their most powerful however, when their energy is vibrant and clear. But since many empaths are unaware of their abilities and unsure of how to traverse the environments they find themselves in, their potent energy can become drained. Therefore, the purpose of this book is to help the empath to heal past hurts, so their energy can reach its highest levels.

Through our childhoods and growing up, we lose so much of our energy and power. But through understanding where this has been lost and by learning more about who we are, we can cleanse ourselves and reclaim this lost energy to live from a new perspective. This helps us to live a happier life and follow our hearts desires. When fully charged and at optimal health, this is when the empath is at their greatest power. Therefore, learning strategies to induce this positive state should become a part of an empaths daily routine.

More and more people are becoming aware of their empathic natures. This topic alone is becoming incredibly popular. At first it was only women who dared to speak out and seek this type of information but now we have people from all walks of life waking up to their true inherent nature. Due to the gender roles we play, men tend to believe that being 'sensitive' is somehow soft or feminine, for this reason this book was written to appeal to the male readers as well as the female. Men are just as likely to possess empathic gifts as women are. But they're sometimes not as accepting of them.

The good news is that the growth in popularity of Empaths is making more information accessible for all of us on how to live a happier life. Through my work as a life coach and spiritual healer, I have come across and dealt with many empaths and sensitives. So in this book I wanted to share what I have learned and the things we need to understand to become emotionally and spiritually stronger.

This book is essentially in two parts, the first part delves into spiritual and emotional healing at its deepest core. I have come to learn that empaths need to be fully healed to reach their potential and I also believe that we can heal from simply reading the right information. When we take in new sources of knowledge and internalize it, it works within our unconscious to help correct the wrongs which helps to heal us emotionally, psychologically and spiritually. The topics in the first half of this title, might be quite heavy reading for some, but this is knowledge that I have personally used to free myself from the hurt of my past, so I urge you to read with an open non-judgmental heart. I believe this information will help give you greater insights, not just into yourself, but others you come into contact with also. The second half of the book is focused more on advanced coping strategies to help keep your body in its optimal state so you can function and perform at your best each day.

Empathy is a true gift however it also comes with a lot of responsibility. To use it to the fullest we have to look after ourselves more than non-empaths. At first it may seem like a drag but once you begin to harness your true empathic power, taking the time to manage your gift will seem an acceptable trade-off.

We should all be able to live free with love in our hearts.

I hope this book helps you to find this love.

The Seven Stages of Empath Development

In this first chapter, you will find the various stages the Empath goes through on their path towards empowerment. These stages can act as a guide for the empath to follow and upon learning what state you're currently at, you can prepare yourself for what is to come while also seeing where you have come from.

'All you need is the plan, the road map, and the courage to press on to your destination'

- Earl Nightingale

1 - Acknowledgement

This originates upon the first realization that you have a sensitive nature. This likely comes from feeling bogged down from others or certain places. Upon discovering your empathic trait, you may feel like it is something you don't want. Newbies will usually try to 'tough it out' or 'deal with it' and believe that this is something they can overcome by simply pushing through whatever is burdening them. In a world where we are taught to be like everyone else, we hate to be different. So, we try to fight it, that's what we are taught by our culture. You might be unaware of what an empath is at this point but you have an inner knowing that you're different from others.

2 - Basic Self-Management

You have begun to reluctantly accept this part of your nature, so you start trying to manage it better. Perhaps you avoid certain people, places or even foods. You may feel you need more time to rest in order to function better. You may have also become aware of the term 'Empath' or 'highly sensitive people' by now and you're gradually coming to terms with this part of yourself.

3 - Investigating Stage

You begin to research, read and watch videos related to energy, sensitivity and coping strategies. You're becoming more consciously aware of the tools available which can help you cope. These initial tools usually come in the form of meditations, crystals or healing practices such as Reiki. Some people at this stage may practice shielding and protecting their aura to keep unwanted energies out. But you're still not jumping with joy at the realization that you have to do these exercises regularly just to be able to function normally. You may even be unsure if these exercises are working but you feel you have no real choice and are probably still feeling down about your trait. It can take a while to completely come to terms with this aspect of our nature. It took me at least a few years. So, don't worry.

4 – The Healing Stage

This is the middle stage of the 7 and the most important in terms of reaching our potential. The number 4 also aligns with the heart chakra which is a place we carry many emotional wounds related to love. At this point you start to understand that you are carrying a lot of pain and hurt with you from the past. You may realize that you need to begin working with your unconscious mind to help you to move into this gift instead of trying to just manage it. Through healing your past hurt, you are able to grow in conscious awareness, which helps you to accept your true nature. This acceptance brings a sense of freedom with increased self-love. You may also feel more in control as you're gradually learning how to deal with external energies. The first half of this book is focused on this important phase of Empath development, this is also often the longest stage for most people.

5 - Deeper Understanding

You are now familiar with the tools and coping strategies for empaths, you are able to turn to them when needed. This helps you handle and manage external energies and not be overwhelmed as much. You are beginning to see your sensitivity as a gift and how it may be of use in daily life. You begin to incorporate these empathic gifts into your life. The healing from the previous stage has helped you get more in tune with yourself and who you really are. Although you still have some difficult moments, you're generally much happier.

6 - Promoting your abilities

You are now able to handle and remain in control with most people and in crowded places. You're able to protect yourself from others emotions and feelings while paying full attention and offering them support if needed. Sometimes you still need to acknowledge if you have picked something up, but you have the skills to transmute any negativity and release it. You're naturally learning to stop taking on others energy from the get go. You are more attuned to the energetic environment around you but can remain present and protected most of the time. You are in control of whether you want to feel other people deeply or if you would rather offer them detached support. You are able to be yourself without becoming overwhelmed.

7 – The Skilled Empath

You're now in complete acceptance of your gift. You see it as a natural part of your being. You may still need to remind yourself to block other energies in certain circumstances such as when meeting new people. But most days you don't even think about your sensitivity as you have learned to manage it unconsciously for the most part. Now you just work to maintain the new healthy balance you have found. You may need to go through a release every now and again which can be achieved through crying or cleansing, which help to remove any energies you have unknowingly absorbed. But most of your attention is now focused on getting more out of your life. You know how to use your empathic gifts to guide you into making the right choices at the right time. Your heart is filled with love and you can extend this to others in a healthy way.

Clairsentience - The Extreme Empath

Clairsentience definition – *'Clear sensation or clear feeling'*

With more and more people coming out with empathic abilities we are beginning to recognize a range in various forms of empathy. On the higher end of the spectrum are those who are called Clairsentients. The clairsentient is the most advanced Empath, in terms of feeling and sensitivity. Whereas the 'regular' empath has the ability to sense and feel others by taking their emotion into their own body. The Clairsentient has the same ability, however, upon taking in others energy they can then instinctively receive information about this persons past or future events and situations.

Empaths can become very connected to the people closet to them, and can even sometimes develop a sixth sense in regard to these people. However, Clairsentients have the ability to use this sixth sense with almost anyone they come into contact with. This of course delves into possessing psychic abilities. This can become very draining if not consciously controlled and contained. Feeling others so deeply can create depression, anxiety and a low energy state. Just as the empath, the

Clairsentient can feel what others are feeling and take the energy or emotions into their bodies. However, they go further and can gain insights into where this emotion come from and why the other person was feeling it. This extra information comes to them through visions, dreams or their intuition. This knowing helps them to understand the other people very deeply.

People possessing these advanced skills may be able to sense and detect energies within other people. They can also pick up on the presence of energies such as spirits. If you can detect energy in an area where no-one is around or have insights about people you barely know than there is a chance you have Clairsentient abilities.

Some of the extra sensory skills of Clairsentients include -

- Thinking about something before it occurs

- Bumping into someone you had just been thinking about

- Correctly predicting what is going to happen in any given situation

- Sensing others presence when they are not there

- Sensing spirits and unseen energies

- Kinesthetic learner. Learn through feeling

Every empath will possess these Clairsentient qualities to a certain degree. Which means we can, if we do wish to, develop these skills further with practice.

Hopefully you now have a basic sense of where you fall on the various stages of Empath development. I believe that we must learn to use this gift if we are to live fully, by choosing to ignore it we will most likely live a stressful and unfulfilling life.

The Empaths Deepest Wound

The information in this chapter will help you to find true self-love which is the first step to living a full life. It is based upon teachings taken from transpersonal psychology, which is also known as 'Spiritual Psychology'. Most of this information is believed to incorporate human psychology with the spiritual experiences of life. It seems that this mid-point is where most of the answers we are looking for may actually lie.

The 'Core Wound' is what I believe to be the root cause of almost all psychological suffering for both empaths and non-empaths. This is the deep-rooted belief that we are not worthy of love which then impacts every area of our lives. Most of us harbor this unconscious belief which stays with us and causes us to live a false life. We then create a false self or mask which we show to the world, which has developed from compensating behaviors to hide the fact that we are unlovable.

Some of us will go through psychotherapy and various healing modalities to overcome unhappiness or dissatisfaction but usually these therapies don't go deep enough to heal the core wounds we carry. The problem with general therapy and self-help, is that it looks to repair or fix the false self or ego. But this is a mask which we developed primarily to compensate for our earliest fears that we were unworthy and separate from love. To experience true emotional growth, we need to stop trying to patch up this false self but instead get to the core of our pain.

For empaths, this core pain can run incredibly deep, which is one of the reasons why traditional healing modalities don't always offer long term reprieve. We have no recollection of our deepest pain since it was created during our earliest years when we experienced the split from unconditional love. This set the foundation for our entire emotional lives. The false self, developed from this split and then worked to hide and repress our original pain into the unconscious, which is why it rarely ever gets discovered.

Our emotional foundation, developed as a result of this split, and become so deeply ingrained within our psychology and biology that we can't even consider being or feeling any different. This negative emotional foundation seems to us to be our truest nature and 'who we really are'. But it is false.

The repressed core pain is the real foundation and sets the tone for our whole lives including our lowest lows and our highest highs. In some way, each experience we have, is somehow compensating for our original wound. Our deepest wound is the cause of all our pain in human life. It is the very first self-concept we have of ourselves and everything else is built and organized on top of it such as our persona and personality.

Therefore, the true steps to healing involves uncovering this pain and working to release its unconscious hold over each part of our life and character. This is the most effective way I have found to help people transform themselves emotionally and psychologically. We can begin to do this by exploring our lives, our relationships, careers, families, dreams and anything else we consider important. Only by paying attention to our behavior and any negative self-talk can we begin to finally free ourselves from the pain which has been with us for so long.

Separation from Unconditional Love

Our deepest wound is experienced when we first realize that we are separate from unconditional love. This initial pain is also labelled the 'narcissistic wound' but in traditional psychology it is believed to develop from the first time a child is made to feel shame which then becomes their deepest belief about themselves. But in actual fact, newer research is suggesting that the original wound occurs earlier than this. It happens when we are babies, when we first experience being separate from the unconditional love which we felt in the womb and from our primary caregiver during the first year of life. In this early state of consciousness, we feel like we are one with everything and surrounded by complete love.

When we first experienced the separation from unconditional love, our primary reaction was fear. We responded to this original trauma by withdrawing ourselves from life. The force of the shock made us become aware that we were separate, we become aware of our body and emotions for the first time. Before this we were unconsciously identified with oneness and love. This shocks us most deeply. The very first thing we feel as a separate human, is a lack of love. This story is painted in the myth of Adam and Eve and their fall from unconsciousness into consciousness.

Compounded with the fact of being empathic, then the shock of separation affects us much more deeply than non-sensitives, as the empaths heightened sense of feeling is wired into their nervous system. This is why sensitives can often struggle their whole life time trying to recover, heal and improve their lives. This initial shock is energetically and emotionally trapped deep within their psyche, nervous system and physical bodies.

We all interpret the original separation from unconditional love in various ways. How we react when we try to move away from the pain of this separation, is what becomes the root cause of all our psychological and emotional pain which follows us through life from then on. Understanding our family and their heritage can give us clues as to what deep negative belief we took on upon first experiencing this painful parting. The reason for this is that we tend to take on pain and hurt which our parents and ancestors were carrying but were unable to heal, so it became genetically programmed into our bodies when we were developing in the womb. Even more so, empaths naturally take on the pain from others and program it into their bodies. If you grow up with a parent who carried a great deal of emotional pain then you may have inherited their pain also.

The False Self-Ego development

Upon realizing that we are separate from the oneness, our young mind develops a deep belief about itself and why it was not worthy of remaining in this loving place. We were babies, therefore did not possess the power of logic and reasoning. The only tool we had is that of feeling, if something didn't feel right then that caused distress to us. Being highly sensitive of course, can make us feel even more discomfort which further enhance any stresses we feel. Here we will explore some of the beliefs that the young mind takes on after this initial split -

I am imperfect

Deep belief - There must be something wrong with me. That is why I cannot feel unconditional love any more.

Persona/Ego development – The character structure which develops from the primary belief that 'I am imperfect', is that I should be better. I should be perfect to prove that there is nothing wrong with me. This person will develop into someone who seeks inner and outer perfection in life. They may also keep their distance from others. But inside can be needy and controlling - desiring to be perfect. They hold the belief that, if they are perfect, they will be healed of their original pain. Since the deepest wound is unconscious, the compensating personality would much rather feel a pain which is distracting and less hurtful. So instead of feeling imperfect, they will feel resentment and envy towards others instead. These negative emotions cover the pain of the original wound that 'I am imperfect'.

I am worthless

Deep belief – The baby internalizes the understanding that I am worthless and have no value. That is why I cannot feel unconditional love any more.

Persona/Ego development - I must prove I have value and that I am not worthless. This person will give too much of themselves to others with the hope of receiving or being valued in return. Deep down they require too much support from others on one hand, but like to appear self-sufficient and independent on the other. To distract themselves from the hurt of being worthless, these people will be become dependent on others or over compensate by becoming excessively independent through external achievements and successes.

I can't do enough

Deep belief - Following the separation from love the young child believes that they cannot do anything in case something bad happens again. They believe that they must have done something wrong for them to be subjected to this fate, therefore they develop the deep-seated belief that it's better not to do anything.

Persona/Ego development - These people grow up with the character structure that they must do more. They can often develop into over achievers. These people can also take on a heightened sense of self and vanity. They avoid the pain of not being able to do enough by compulsive over doing.

I am alone

Deep belief - This person develops the belief that they are alone. Once the connection to oneness through the primary caregiver is lost, the separation makes them feel isolated.

Persona/Ego development - They will avoid being alone by trying to connect with others. Through connection with others, these people gain a sense of validation. However, they constantly need to be in contact with others to distract themselves from their deepest pain. They also avoid their pain through excessive fear, anxiety, self-doubt or they may over compensate by presenting themselves as strong and in control of everything.

These are just some of the ways in which the young child's mind will interpret the wound of separation. The child at this age cannot speak or think clearly, so they rely on their feelings and emotions to guide them. But their incorrect interpretation of reality becomes the foundation of their persona/ego. Over time and as the years pass by, this persona becomes solidified and stronger within the character structure, until the individual believes this false self to be 'who they really are'. The separation from unconditional love, is one of the reasons that many people struggle with finding a deep sense of self-love within themselves.

Healing the Spilt

This theory predisposes that when we come into life on Earth, we are a soul which prior to life on Earth came from a place of oneness and absolute love. This soul comes to Earth in order to learn, grow and expand. But in order to do so, it first had to become separate and then find its way back to unconditional love.

This spilt is a huge shock to the baby, who has come from love to a world which can be anything but. Unfortunately, most people on our planet are wearing masks which are not authentic, just to compensate for childhood pains. Deep down they don't feel a profound unconditional love for themselves. The world is full of egos of people who are afraid to face their deepest hurts and pains which paradoxically would set them free, but instead they unconsciously over compensate.

Cause of the Deepest Wound

From a biological understanding, upon realizing that we are separate and spilt away from unconditional love, we receive a shock to the nervous system. Which of course, in empaths is highly sensitized already. This shock happens at a time where the mind and body are most fragile. Taking on this pain so early in development is what engrains it so deeply. It is believed this spilt occurs around 6 months to 1 years of age and in some cases even in the womb before birth.

The belief we take on about ourselves upon this separation helps to cover the trauma and shock of the division from oneness. Immediately following the split, we are first aware that something feels different and not as loving. Then it is only when we reach the verbal stage, our thinking mind develops and creates an inner story to explain to ourselves why we're not worthy of love. This compounds upon the original foundation of pain to form the character of the individual. The harder the spilt is felt, the more emotional problems one will experience in life. Empaths will generally feel the pain of the spilt deeper due to their natural sensitivity.

Our deepest wound essentially controls how the ego develops. This hurt works to filter our reality and builds defenses within the ego structure so we don't ever have to face the pain of separation again, as we originally did. Since it was so hurtful to us as babies, the thought of re-experiencing it psychologically and emotionally is too overwhelming. The ego persona controls who we become and keeps us safe but prevents us from experiencing life fully in all of its glory.

I believe that if the young child experiences healthy loving parenting following the split, they can remain in touch with the oneness and love as they grow up into individuals. This is what helps creates psychologically healthy people with high self-esteem. However, if the environment is hostile and any abuse is witnessed or experienced then any contact with unconditional love can be lost all together.

Our sensitive nervous systems are programmed early in our development to protect us no matter what. This safety-first measure means we are never able to free ourselves from this internal prison to experience the truth of who we really are. Most people will have to suffer a breakdown or hit a real low point in order to learn that they can get through it and find the lost love within themselves. An external trigger will usually come in the form of a break-up, some kind of loss or even a drastic financial problem. Only then will people allow themselves to truly feel the pain which they have been carrying in their hearts for so long. Only then can they learn to embrace the pain through their loving conscious awareness. By opening ourselves up to experiencing more vulnerability we allow love to shine through our pain.

As the persona/ego begins to form so early in our development, we wrongly believe this is who we truly are. But this 'ego' developed from a painful experience and not from a place of love. Most people on our planet have no idea that they have a true self under their ego and therefore never get close to uncovering it. The ego, of course, acts as a mask hiding our deepest pain and the fear that we are unlovable as who we really are. The last time we were authentic, we experienced the pain of separation. This formed a strong neurological connection that being your true self results in deep emotional pain, which then deters us away from our truth. When we avoid our deepest wounds, it can lead us into a life long journey of therapy, self-help work, spiritual practices and various other healings. We may go around in circles trying to get to the bottom of our issues. We may even experience some short-term relief but then usually another problem arises. This is because we are attempting to fix the false ego self. Self-development and certain psychotherapeutic treatments will attempt to create change in the ego structure which only reinforces the initial wound of our separation.

The pain from our earliest developmental stages, becomes embedded deep within our unconscious psyche and physiology in the form of trapped energy and emotions. It then continues to control us from behind the scenes, running in the background and governing most of our life. Because of this deep level programming, we will often go through life unable to obtain what we want, to live the life we desire or to even find a suitable loving partner. This is because we cannot attract something to us which isn't a vibrational match.

This is especially relevant for empaths who naturally vibrate at a higher frequency, this means they attract similar vibrational matches towards them much easier. But if they are vibrating the deep belief that they are unworthy of love, then attracting what they want can become almost impossible. The empath becomes like a beckon transmitting a signal that deep down they feel unworthy. This transmission can only bring back something of a similar frequency. For

We cannot change ourselves or our circumstances by merely wishing or dreaming. Of course, the ego will try to portray that it is worthy and deserving. But this conscious attempt will not be powerful enough to overthrow the deep-rooted belief picked up during the spilt from unconditional love, which will always win in proving externally that we are unworthy. For instance, you may consciously feel you want a romantic partner but will likely continue to attract the wrong people if you're not in touch with your self-love. The persona/ego cannot let go or make itself vulnerable enough to experience the original trauma again. Which if experienced fully, would allow healing to occur. We tend to trust in our ego and its drive, for bringing us what we want. When in actual fact, it usually keeps whatever we desire, out of our grasp. Our deep-seated beliefs which formed the foundation of the personality have been running autonomously for so many years and as a result have developed so much strength and momentum that they will always out muscle the egos choices.

It is not possible for our unconscious and our conscious awareness to compete fairly. One is a powerful monster which is constantly being reinforced and made stronger through our long-standing character and behavior, whereas the ego is simply insignificant and puny in comparison. Our conscious thinking mind makes up around 5% of our total programming which clearly shows that wishful thinking alone will not suffice to help you to live a happier and more fulfilled life. To do this we need to harness the power of the unconscious, where all the pain and hurt lies. Once we can traverse and conquer it, the future for our lives becomes ever promising.

To develop unconditional love for ourselves we must first begin to understand the beliefs we took on during the separation from love. We then need to try to reconnect with the sense of love which we felt before we took on the false understanding that we were unworthy. Through practices such as meditation (explained in later chapters) we can reconnect to this unconditional love which has been with us all along. It has just been hidden away and covered up. Once we begin to experience it again we gradually start to incorporate it into our conscious awareness and life for good.

Since the nervous system develops so early in childhood, in response to not being loved, it is unable to open itself up to feelings of unconditional love. The persona we carry does whatever it can to keep our inner pain hidden while also attempting to prove it is wrong. This is what leads to over compensating behaviors within the personality. However, for the deep hurt to remain it needs to feel the resulting behaviors which were built in response to it. For instance, if we feel unworthy, we will take action to prove our worth. This helps to keep us feeling safe by making things seem familiar and known. The human mind is naturally threatened when presented by something new or unknown. However, within this feeling of a lack of love, is the doorway for us to return to this state of bliss and self-love. We can heal our wound by trusting ourselves to feel and sense the pain of the original spilt. This shows us where the emptiness lies and also where the portal to healing exists.

This loss of love, also resides within our physical bodies. Empaths should try to become more aware and attuned to their physical bodies and the sensations they feel within them. If you can sit in meditation with inner body awareness, you will begin to sense where this lack of love and emptiness resides within the body. Upon sensing this place, start to consciously bring unconditional love back into your being and body. The first step is to acknowledge and feel the lack, only then can it be filled with love.

How to heal the Split

Here are directions to help you begin healing the spilt and its resulting wound.

1) Understand the initial belief - Try to discover what understanding you took on once you felt the split from oneness. It may take you some time to figure this out but trust your empathic instincts, they will usually guide you and present you with the truth. Refer to the descriptions above for the most common beliefs we feel upon the spilt.

2) As mentioned, pay attention to your physical body. Where do you sense a feeling of lack? While thinking about your initial belief, bring your awareness into the body. Try to see how you may close down or hide certain parts of your body out of fear of reexperiencing pain. If you struggle with locating the pain, become aware of how you feel when someone violates you. Any emotional intrusion will often be felt in the body, this will be close to where your deep wound resides.

3) Stay with your fear - Once you have sensed your deep pain try to stay with it. Keep your awareness in this space for as long as you can. Do not try to change it in to something else but simply stay with it in the moment. The pain of the wound wants to be experienced and acknowledged, which is a crucial step to healing. Try to

accept it and show it loving kindness for it has been with you for so long and was only trying to protect you. Do not judge or resent it.

4) Feel the pain. Open yourself up to the wound. Try breathing deeply into this area for as long as possible. Remember to see the pain as neutral, neither good or bad. With regular practice this becomes easier to endure.

5) Reconnect to your loving essence. How does love feel in your body? When you think about love where does it reside? Try to sense this loving feeling in your heart. With attention and commitment this unconditional love will begin to grow. With practice, you can dial into this love frequency and then allow it into your whole body and specifically the area where your deep wound resides.

Fear

The first natural defense mechanism we have as babies is to close ourselves off using our bodies to protect us from feeling vulnerable. Therefore, as adults, whenever we sense a feeling of either psychological or emotional vulnerability, our bodies respond by triggering a fear response. This reaction prevents us from re-experiencing the pain which wants to be acknowledged and felt. The pain which we refused to face when it originally occurred does not go away. When we continue to avoid our painful feelings, our growth will usually take on a repeating pattern where we continually go over the same things again and again. This can continue for years with no reprieve. Our fears repeatedly come up, as they are hardwired into our biology, which continue to organize and strengthen the negative beliefs. Every time we fail to acknowledits ge a negative feeling, we strengthen its hold over us. Only when we come to realize that our pain and vulnerability must be felt can we begin to gradually release it.

Trying to heal and working on ourselves excessively can feel like we are doing something positive and it is not a bad thing. However, I have witnessed many people turn into 'self-help junkies'. They fall into the trap of believing that if they continually work on themselves they will eventually find happiness or some fulfilment but instead they usually spend years going around in circles. This is simply their egos organizing principle running in the background, needing something to keep it going. Therefore, the ego becomes addicted to doing 'inner work'. We think it is helping us, when in fact it may not be as beneficial as it first seems. The ego tricks us into thinking that one day it will be healed. The problem is, that the ego is a bottomless pit which can never be fully healed or filled. The only real solution is to go beyond the ego.

Most people cannot imagine releasing their character or the personality they think they are, for if they did, then they may fail to exist? Therefore, the deep emotional wounds continue to survive because they are intertwined with the ego, which we are constantly trying to heal and repair. It is like carrying a bottle of water with a hole in it, once the hole is patched up another hole appears and so on. Until we are forever trying to patch up this bottle to prevent leaks. But we can never stop the leakage.

Out of fear of losing our character or personality we continue to keep our pain alive. Each time we begin to get within range of our true loving self, fear rears its head and we struggle to let go, because our true inner essence doesn't have the same organizing and 'safety' which the ego has given us for so long. In fact, going deeper into our true spiritual core can seem empty and scary because it seems unknown. But we have simply just forgotten about it.

The human nervous system houses the ego and all of its defenses. This illustrates why it can take empaths such a long time to heal. The ego resides in the same place as our sensitivity. The only difference is that our empathetic abilities were genetic, whereas the ego and its developments were learned and programmed into the nervous system afterwards. Since the ego was created early in our lives and helped keep us safe, it has an amazing desire to remain since it developed our whole biological and psychological organizing structure (behavior). We naturally think the ego is just in our mind, but in fact the whole biology houses the ego, and it will do whatever it can to feel stable just to keep us from re-experiencing our deep wounds. Our programming therefore, wants to prove that our original belief is true. Then reality reflects back to us, the deep belief that we are worthless and we spend our whole lives unconsciously reinforcing it.

The unconscious drive to prove the initial belief to be true is overwhelmingly powerful. Any attempts through conscious effort to portray 'positive' or opposing qualities are weak in comparison to the unconscious. Our initial deep belief or wound is relentless and since it has developed with our biological ego defense system it works like a non-stop machine. The only way to overcome it, is to finally pull the plug on it. Otherwise there is no way to prevent this unstoppable machine running continuously for the rest of your life.

Self-love

Unconditional love is how we are born, it is our truest nature. The ego character structure develops afterwards. But we can get back to this through commitment, dedication and a willingness to remain present with our hurt. From this place, we gradually begin to allow the larger unifying principle of unconditional love to move into the background of our awareness and our lives.

Once this deep love comes into our life, we become much more stable. External circumstances and things which affected us emotionally in the past begin to lose their power over us because we are now being governed by something much bigger and authentic.

We then become more consciously aware when our emotional pain is triggered. As we begin to reside in unconditional self-love, the false belief that we are bad or unworthy gradually dissolves from the forefront or our awareness. It loses its control over our personality and slowly a new creative character starts to emerge.

Through commitment and will, we can learn to stay with whatever emotion arises within us. Then with time, the potency of these negative emotions begins to reduce. We may still feel overwhelmed when our pain is triggered but we will be able to detach and stop it from taking over us. This is because our inherent true loving nature has been restored and so naturally dissolves the pain of negative emotions. We become even more aware and see things which we have never seen before. In other words, we develop a new deeper perspective. When this new perception is combined with the gifts of empathy we become truly powerful and from this place we can start to change not only our own lives, but positively impact the world with our true power.

Many of us go through healing and feel we have made good progress but often times similar or new issues continue to emerge. It seems as though our healing never ends. But, I am happy to say that when people have become more aware of the dynamics of how their ego operates, they have experienced a big shift on their journey towards self-healing once and for all.

Although traditional self-healing doesn't heal our deepest wounds, as it usually works on the ego, it does help to make us psychologically stronger. So, all the work which was done prior does serve a purpose. It gives us the courage to face our truth of unconditional love. With the courage and strength we have developed, we can teach ourselves to remain open to all of our emotions and feelings. So that we do not shut ourselves off when we feel vulnerable, but instead go into the feeling and pain. This awareness of our inner world allows us to acknowledge and process all the emotions we feel while moving closer to our essence.

Almost every experience is engrained into the mind and body. For empaths, this programming runs very deep. But learning to remain present with your feelings with unconditional loving awareness regardless of what is coming up is the only spiritual practice you need to do in order to heal. The fight, flight or freeze responses are programmed into all of our psychological defenses. We heal when the awareness of our loving presence becomes bigger than the degree of pain. When we can release the emotion, these stress defenses fall away and we grow in conscious awareness.

By finally overcoming the false self, we learn that we don't 'lose' who we thought we were. In fact, all the skills and traits which we had developed get transferred to a much more powerful aspect of ourselves. We are essentially still the same people but we see life differently which means we also experience more.

True emotional healing requires that we stay with the process. This can take time to achieve, as we must deal with each layer, one at a time. When we are ready for the next level then we will become aware of it. Sometimes we may need to stay with certain emotions for longer periods of time than others but eventually each emotions energy will disperse with our loving awareness and return to our essence. Giving us more energy to live life.

The False Self

Following the spilt from unconditional love we enter a second stage of development. This phase is important in determining how we will develop and solidifies the character structure in the individual even further.

Most of us create a 'false' self or a persona in certain situations. Sometimes this is done consciously, as it helps us to deal with situations. Take for example, your job or career. You may have to present yourself as someone professional to be successful in your role. This is acceptable to a degree. But some people can forget the roles they are playing and think they're the mask. This is one of the reasons some of us are anxious, introverted or lack confidence. Somewhere along the line, an authentic part of ourselves went into hiding.

A mask develops as a basic sense of protection, empaths often do it, to feel non-threatened and safe. Most of us are aware when we are putting on an act under certain circumstances. However, some people take on a false self and become unaware and unconscious of the mask they are wearing. They mistake this false mask as who they really are.

This false self usually develops in early childhood following the split from oneness. If the child was loved unconditionally then they will have remained in touch with the truth that they are worthy. But others may have found themselves in difficult environments. For some reason, many empaths and sensitives I have dealt with have experienced a bumpy childhood. Sometimes I believe it is the empaths life's purpose to experience and transmute pain. However, this is not to suggest that every empath has a difficult up-bringing, but it is very common.

In a less than adequate childhood, the young empath may witness or experience physical or emotional abuse. Following the split and the sense they are separate, they need a safe environment to help them to remain in contact with their truth. When this doesn't happen however, their true self goes into hiding as it doesn't feel safe in a hostile environment and a false self-develops in its place.

The false self can also develop to please the family. This is something I have witnessed with many empaths. Due to their heightened sensitivity, they feel the fear and turmoil in their environment much more deeply. Out of this anxiety a false self is created. When this happens at such an early age, the false persona becomes so well constructed that it becomes accepted by the family that helped create it in the first place. Then this false self is continually reinforced and continues to gain validation from the family environment which spawned it, until eventually the true self is completely forgotten. The true self becomes so well hidden that we cannot find it, it is lost to us. It remains elusive as it carries the initial fear and pain which we were so frightened of experiencing.

Seeking out the true self will bring up the pain and hurt from the past. It can also impact your current position in the family and environment because it may make you go against the status quo of the family. These are important points to consider. To really find ourselves we must also understand the sacrifices we must make.

The foundation of the false self is weak, as it was built in response to external circumstances which we interpreted as fearful. As babies our judgement was not the best and being overly sensitized to the environment. If the environment was negative and bad, we felt it was because we were bad. A young child, doesn't possess logic and insight therefore they unconsciously blame themselves for what they perceive. So, they develop a character which they feel would be more accepted and strong enough to deal with any difficulties.

The false self is also known as the 'idealized self' which develops because our true self feels too weak, inadequate and overwhelmed in the situation it finds itself in. This causes us to create a self which we felt at the time, was stronger and more suitable to the environment. A self that is better able to cope, avoid pain and feel safer. Some of us start to idealize this false self. For example, controlling or manipulating other people becomes 'cleverness'. This fake self, steps in when our true self is unable to cope.

Feeling our truth can hurt due to the pain it carries. The pain hurts too much. The pain must mean I am bad. The false self takes the place of the true self like an actor takes over the true identity of the person. Its acts as a smoke screen to avert people away from the true pained self.

Most of us create a false self in certain circumstances, in order to keep our deepest emotions under control, so we don't express them inappropriately. This is normal. But the problem arises when we mistake the false self as who we really are. But when wearing a mask all of the time, eventually holes begin to show. Also, carrying the weight around of a false self is heavy and it robs the person of life energy.

The false self also hinders the growth of the authentic true self. Through us, the false self learns to build its self-up, develop confidence, strength and acceptance while the authentic self withers-away starving for attention and acknowledgement.

Why Does This Happen?

We would like to think, being at home and with family is the one place we can truly be ourselves. But what if we didn't feel like that when we were young children? What if it was too frightening? Maybe our sensitive little body couldn't bare negative emotions and the energy which was inherent in the atmosphere. As babies, we can't speak or understand what's going on around us. Our minds aren't developed enough. The only way we can gauge our environment is through our feelings. We trust them and go with them. Whatever we feel we believe to be true. As we grow up into adults we begin to stop trusting our feelings as much and instead rely more on our logic. But learning to get back in touch your feelings is an incredibly powerful way to live a worthwhile life.

The development of a false self is also commonly seen in alcoholic families or families where the dynamics were not balanced. This can also be witnessed in rich, overly strict and religious households. In these dysfunctional families, the young child learns to adapt itself and not to express what they see going on around them. If Dad drinks a lot, it often doesn't get talked about but instead gets brushed under the carpet. But the energetic footprint is always present and felt by the empath. By unconsciously avoiding the reality of the situation, everyone involved loses sight of themselves. If they did dare to acknowledge the reality of what was going on, they may be shamed, hurt or feel bad about their judgement. So instead they simply copy the others around them and avoid seeing the reality.

Not feeling safe enough to be open about what is going on in their immediate environment, the child abandons themselves and avoids feeling. This causes the child to live an emotional lie. They are afraid that if the truth is acknowledged then others and themselves will be hurt. So instead the whole family unit unconsciously works together to maintain the status quo to appear like a healthy and functional household. We have to disown ourselves to protect this fake image and avoid the truth.

The tricky thing about confronting parts of ourselves which are not authentic is that they have means of hiding and tricking us into believing the illusion is real. The false self doesn't want to feel the pain which is underlying its existence. Therefore, it will do whatever it can to avoid it. Just as we did as a young child. This false self was intelligently built by a young creative mind, so undoing its hold now can become a challenge unless you can gain brand new insights and learn to trust in your empathic intuition.

When those who have a false self, go through healing or some type of therapy they will likely experience a stage of feeling extremely vulnerable. This is due to the fact they are removing the coping strategies they had taken on. This exposes the wound and the hurt which they had been hiding all along. But with this insight they can start to build new emotional habits and behaviors along with giving healthier coping mechanisms the chance to develop. Then they can finally begin to live within their truth where greater happiness and fulfillment lies.

You may find these first few chapters heavy going. If you do, please take the time to walk away from this and take the time to process what you have read. The reason I felt it was important to include this chapter is due to the increasing number of empaths I have met in my work, who were traumatized as young child and the effect on them stays with them. By learning more about our conditioning and inherent nature we can learn to live life more comfortably.

Repressed Sexuality and the Empath

The purpose of this chapter is to help the empath to get more in tune with their humanity. Being an empath is seen as a spiritual subject and because of this we can start to lose sight of our animal nature. It is important that we try to live authentically and owning our sexuality is one of the most powerful ways to do that. This is not to suggest we become promiscuous or careless with our sexuality.

We may not realize it but as a society and culture we are sexually repressed. In fact, famous psychologist Sigmund Freud claimed that sexual repression was the main problem behind all the psychological issues we face in modern society. It is one of the longest standing taboos of human culture. The truth is that sex is neither good nor bad. It is completely natural and normal. Without it, life would cease to exist. How can we shame and disregard something which is responsible for the survival of all life?

This issue can become even more difficult to deal with for empaths due to their sensitive natures. This aspect of themselves can be hidden away very deeply, as sensitives tend to repress quite strongly. But by beginning to learn how to embrace this part of ourselves, this can be one of the keys to living a full balanced mature happy life. In fact, problems with repressed sexuality can create any number of emotional and physical issues including depression, anxiety and low-self-esteem, among others.

For many thousands of years, we have been on the receiving end of religious dogma telling us that sex is bad and forbidden. Religions set the tone of life by preaching to us what is 'right' and what is 'wrong', these teachings developed the foundation of our culture. Some people have suggested that those who controlled the religions had an agenda and intentionally choose to repress sexuality as a means of controlling the masses.

Nonetheless, these programming's become deeply ingrained within our personal and the collective unconscious of mankind which prevents us from truly letting ourselves go and enjoying our true human nature fully. Sex is completely natural and healthy in nature and wildlife. So why should humans see it any differently?

Our sexuality is as normal as sleeping, eating, drinking and all other natural human behaviors. Sexual energy is the life force which makes everything come alive, so to deny this can be awfully harmful. The sexual repression that is promoted by religion and culture at large is further compounded by the households we grew up in. If they were either very conservative or religious then it is likely that your deep-seated beliefs about sex are incredibly dysfunctional. As young children, we are taught to listen to others so we begin to lose trust in our own bodies and wrongly place too much trust into the beliefs we are fed.

Try to remember what significance sex held for your family. Perhaps they were somewhat open about it or maybe it was incredibly uncomfortable. Some of the beliefs we pick up about sex can be either very obvious such as 'don't have sex before marriage' or can be subtle and understated, such as when there is no mention of sex whatsoever.

Media also plays an increasingly important role, on one hand we are exposed to semi naked models through advertising campaigns and social media yet on the other hand we are conditioned from an early age to treat sex as an unspoken taboo. These contradictions and conflicts make it difficult for us to heal from our pasts and learn how to own all of ourselves. It creates a spilt within us, as the information we are receiving is not congruent.

Empaths can sometimes have strange sexual behaviors which are usually a result of this repression. As mentioned prior, an empath will usually over compensate due to their sensitive nature so the problem of repression can sometimes be worse.

Our culture also tends to find it acceptable to be exposed to violence and aggression but uncomfortable when presented with something of a sexual nature. We have learned to allow in one part of life, but not others. This leads to an imbalance within the human psyche. Sexual energy is one of the most powerful aspects of being human so to repress something so inherent will only cause disturbances in our well-being. Whatever we repress gets twisted into something negative if we don't allow it healthy expression. Repressed energy, can come out through our fears and feelings of anxiety, while distorting the true essence of our sexuality. Which then comes out in unhealthy and dysfunctional ways. Our sexual nature colors each part of our lives from our most intimate relationships to our day to day interactions.

Some of the common beliefs people pick up about sex include –

Masturbation is forbidden

Homosexuality is evil

Sex before marriage makes you bad and is wrong

Sex is unnatural

Learning these false beliefs as young children leads to a split in the child. If we ever feel curious about our bodies and sex but are told it is wrong, we start to believe that we are wrong for thinking and feeling this way. But we can't help it, we are just exploring our feelings. This causes us to disassociate from ourselves and a powerful part of who we are goes into hiding out of fear of being shamed again.

Some of modern society is gradually beginning to open up to sexuality, however this isn't enough to override the many years of cultural sexual repression which began with the ancient religions. Some of the worlds cultures are incredibly sexually repressed therefore it is not surprising that these countries are some of the most violent as well. When we do not allow our most powerful instincts expression, unfortunately they do not go away and instead show themselves in other dysfunctional ways.

Certain traditions of spirituality teach us that sexual energy is essentially a life force or spiritual energy.

Religion should have had the same view and created a sacred way for people to express their sexuality in a healthy way, this would have reduced the amount of problems we have been faced with throughout human history. But instead sexuality was repressed into the unconscious where it becomes dark and seeks expression through predatory instincts which leads to the abuse of others. Sexual repression is one of the reason pornography has become so popular.

Through healing and accepting your sexuality you can begin to live with more freedom, creativity and life energy. Think back if you ever felt bad or guilty about your body's natural urges. Many of us were shamed whenever we felt or expressed our sexuality. We don't come into the world knowing what is socially acceptable and what isn't. So, we take in and believe whatever we are taught. The reactions we were faced with by our parents are what shapes our thoughts and behaviors around sexuality.

Empaths are naturally born with a feeling and sensual side, but this shaming can leave them with deep wounds and beliefs about their sexuality. When an empath is made to feel bad it cuts deeper and therefore the wounds are more difficult to heal. But we can begin to rewrite old programming's by understanding that sexuality is part of our nature and something which should be embraced. Through understanding our current beliefs about sex, we begin to see how they may be wrong and see sex as something natural and innocent.

This may go against what we were made to believe but this life force energy can give us so much if we are willing to release it and allow it in. When sexual energy is severely repressed or controlled it can become dark and twisted which can make people carry out terrible acts. But if we could all openly accept our natural humanity, then acts of sex related and violent crime would probably fall dramatically, as a result.

If you have been a victim of any type of sexual abuse I would urge you to seek professional help. The trauma of such an act can severely disrupt an empaths ability to live life fully and enjoy their own sexuality. The empath will experience this trauma so deeply that it will become engrained within their nervous system and body. This often leads to a shutting down of their feelings. This switching off is usually an unconscious act from the victims, as a tool for not feeling the abuse they are being subjected too. But it also leaves them with an inability to feel their own emotions.

Sexual abuse and crime is rooted in our sexually repressed culture. Since so many of us are sexually repressed, it creates an energetic imbalance collectively and individually, which seeks release through crime and disruption. These terrible acts, lead to further cultural sexual repression which creates even more lonely, sexually repressed people and therefore the crimes and abuse continue. Interestingly, the world produces phallic symbols of sexual repression through weapons of war such as bullets, guns, missiles and the like. These things are all anti-life.

If we don't want to die of starvation, we eat food. But we don't always treat our sexuality in the same way. We all have a hunger to experience intimacy, to be touched and caressed. But, we are so sexually repressed (particularly empaths) that we don't allow ourselves to really enjoy and let go into the experiences of our physical bodies.

We can become more open though. If you do not have a sexual partner, then try to get a regular massage which can help soothe you providing it is conducted in a caring way. Our children should be made to feel comfortable with being caressed by us in a loving way through acts of love such as cuddles and pats on the back. Sexual education should start in the home at a relatively young age so that young people understand that sex is something which is natural.

Some people will disagree with this idea of making children aware of sex at an early age, as they believe it could sexualize the child and as a result they will begin to think about it more. But the truth is that we only obsess about the things we repress or don't acknowledge. Such as the things which we don't fully accept or give an outlet.

Sexual Healing

Here are some steps you can begin to take in order to start healing your damaged sexuality. This will allow you to experience much more joy and fulfillment through sex and life.

1) Childhood

Begin healing your sexuality by looking back to your childhood and exploring the beliefs which you picked up. What were your parent's thoughts around sexuality? Were you raised in a strict or religious household where sex was a big taboo? Would your parents try to make you feel bad about it? Or perhaps they were open and accepting of the natural human instincts.

By learning more about our early programming we can begin to understand the beliefs we hold to help determine just how sexually repressed we might be. Also by adding the fact of our empathic nature into the equation, we will have experienced our parent's rules and teachings more deeply which has the potential to repress us even deeper.

2) Self-Acceptance

Learning to accept ourselves fully, in body, mind and spirit can help free us from sexual repression. Through complete acceptance of our animalistic nature we stop feeling bad about our feelings or being sorry for who we essentially are. Once we accept our sexuality we can begin to use its inherent power to drive and fuel us towards reaching our life goals.

Without full self-acceptance, we are unable to accept others fully either because we don't feel worthy. If you're guilty of taking blame from others or lacking assertiveness, this is an unconscious tendency of shaming ourselves, which is also a by-product of sexual repression. We recreate the shame and guilt we felt in childhood through our adult behavior. A lack of assertiveness in our daily lives shows that we are afraid to fulfill our own needs. Especially getting our sexual needs met. By learning to express our natural need for closeness and intimacy leads to us being able to express ourselves more fully in other areas of our lives. Non-assertive behavior comes from the deep-seated belief that we must be good so that others accept us. This can also be an extension of sexual repression where we were taught to believe that sex was bad, so we did what we could to be good.

3) Journaling

I am a huge advocate of writing about how we feel each day. Through this simple act, we can begin to process and heal ourselves in various ways while also understanding ourselves more deeply. Some people like to write each day, others prefer to write whenever they sense something significant. The important thing is that you make it a regular practice and tune into your feelings.

4) Communicate Your Sexuality

By getting more in touch with what you like and do not like during sex, lets you experience more of yourself in a healthy and enjoyable way. To do this, you must take your awareness deeply into the body and sense how various sensations feel to you. Some people like to use sex as a form of meditation, where they allow their thoughts to dissipate and instead focus on the feelings and sensations being experienced.

With practice, you'll learn to express what you like and as a result become more attuned to yourself. This simple expression of your needs, will help improve your assertiveness and confidence outside of the bedroom, while making you more attractive to your significant other.

5) Sexual Healing Arts

We are all naturally creative. Humans have the inherent ability to create. Whether that is a child, a relationship, a business or whatever. This natural creativity is our sexual energy, which we can tap into through drawing or painting with a sense of passion. Grab some crayons, a paint brush or coloring pens and see what comes out of you. Empaths should be able to go deeply into their creativity. Just as they naturally feel more, this also gives them the ability to go deeper within to draw out something magnificent.

6) Self-Care

Taking care of ourselves comes from the inherent belief that we are worthy of care and love. This also allows us to feel more desirable which helps attract others to us. True intimacy and compatibility doesn't come from physical beauty (although this helps initially) but instead from ones' true essence. By loving ourselves deeply, warts and all, we can begin to harness the depth and power of our natural sexuality. Take care of yourself through eating healthy foods, exercising regularly, washing and cleaning yourself. But do not carry these acts out just for validation from others, instead do them out of a deep love for yourself.

When we start to feel genuine self-love, our heart begins to open, then we naturally draw more love into our lives.

Emotionally wounded empaths often struggle with self-love, if this is you, I suggest taking a long period of time to work on loving yourself unconditionally. Try taking a whole year on just learning how to love yourself more. This practice alone will heal most emotional issues.

Self-love is something which I personally practiced with commitment and by the time 1 year had passed my life had completely transformed into something which represented the deep love I had for myself. No matter where you're starting from, with a willingness to heal you can improve your situation drastically. If there was only one thing we should work on to improve our lives, then I would advise people to concentrate upon self-love as it bleeds into every other aspect of life, through building self-esteem and confidence.

Sexual Intimacy

Empaths and sensitives should pay extra care to who they share themselves with. Close intimate contact intertwines the aura and energy of one person with the other person's aura. These are strong connections. It is the closest we can get to another physically, which brings us closer energetically also. The problem for empaths is that they easily pick up negative energy and emotions from the other during sexual contact. Especially if the other person doesn't practice cleansing, balancing and clearing their own energy. Empaths pick up unwanted energy from simply passing people in the street, so just think how long negative sexual energy may stay with them for?!

Regular cleansing is a must for all empaths, as picking up unwanted energy is as simple as picking up dust. Cleansing our energy is similar to washing the body. If we don't wash we get dirty which allows germs to grow that eventually causes illness and disease. The same is true with our energetic space, if we don't cleanse it of negative energies then our aura becomes negative and dirty. We then attract similar things to us. I like to call this spiritual cleansing, and I believe in the future more and more people will do it. The later chapters will discuss how we can keep our energy cleaner and clearer.

The more times the empath has sex with the same partner, the more their two auras gel together. But those who have numerous sexual partners often carry negative, confused or clouded energy around with them. By carrying a lot of negative energy, we attract more of it to us. Having sex is essentially an exchange of energy between two people.

Any kind of sexual intimacy combines the energy of both people, we absorb some of theirs and vice versa. This also works favorably as well, if we have sexual contact with someone who is positive and loving, then we will experience an uplift but if they're negative or low energy then we will suffer, while they take away our high positive energy. Sleeping with a regular partner means the energies will intertwine but in a much more balanced and healthy way. In this scenario, we learn how to accommodate each other's energy.

So, the next time you decide to be intimate with someone new, qualify them first. But try not to judge. You're simply putting your well-being first and this is not an excuse to look down on others. We know that empaths pick up so much, very easily, so sex can really drag an empath down if they are not more conscious about the close company they keep. This topic is covered in even greater depth in the teachings of Tantric Sex.

Never sleep with someone you wouldn't want to be! This is an empowering rule to live by to help keep you clear.

Healing Methods for Sensitives

Healing from our past hurts is a noble pursuit and I don't believe we have to spend hundreds or even thousands of dollars on seeking professional help. In our households, we have access to everyday tools which we can use to help us to heal and transform ourselves. This chapter is dedicated to helping teach you some ways to move forward.

Healing Water

A Japanese researcher by the name of Dr. Masaru Emoto experimented with water and discovered that human consciousness could influence the molecular structure of water. Through his experiments, he proved that sending positive words, affirmations, prayers, feelings and visualizations into water, created beautifully formed crystals within it. These tiny crystals were only visible through a microscope. However, the opposite was also true, negative words and thoughts caused disturbing and disfigured images within the water. With this profound discovery, he understood that we could use water in more ways than we had originally thought.

When we consider that the human body is predominately made up of water, it shows the scope of this profound discovery and the possibilities of using water to change and heal ourselves. As we know, Empaths take on others emotions and energy into their bodies easily, this impacts them physiologically and emotionally. But we can begin to overwrite this by working with water. Water is one of the most important elements we need as humans to survive. It is not surprising then that 70% of the human body is made up of water.

Water has the chemical structure named H20. Science has proven that the H20 molecules can arrange themselves in specific ways depending upon their environment. So, water will structure its molecules around whatever it is surrounded by. This is important to consider, for instance, if the water is surrounded by positivity and love, it will arrange itself accordingly.

The water in our bodies energetically adapts itself to how we feel and what we pick up. If we carry wounds or negative emotions, the water will adapt to this vibration.

As we take in more water, it will naturally structure itself in this negative way.

There is a simple spiritual practice which we can begin to do each and every day to help us overwrite the hurt we carry in our physiology. Begin by taking a glass of clear water. Place both hands around the glass and start to focus upon someone you love deeply. This can be anyone such as a family member, friend, partner, or anything that helps you to experience strong feelings of love.

Concentrate upon these feelings of love in your body, where can you feel them? Next begin to transfer the emotions through your hands and into the glass you're holding. This will project the loving vibrations into the water in the glass. Visualize this love flowing through you and into the water. It is best to try and do this for at least a few minutes. It is generally considered the longer you can do this, the better. Finally, complete the exercise by drinking the water.

Commit to this practice and do it at least once each day. Over time you will start to restructure the water within your body. This will help rid you of negative vibrations and resistance but program you with loving feelings for yourself and others.

Most of us drink tap or bottled water, we don't know where it has been or who has handled it. Therefore, we have no idea what vibrations the water is carrying.

With this subtle practice, we can start to take our power back and through regular use begin growing into love. If you have suffered from abuse or from a lack of self-love then drinking this treated water can have a profound impact. Some people report having huge physical and psychological breakdowns from this practice especially if they have been stuck in a place of fear (the opposite of love).

Other tips include, writing positive words on your bottle of water. Any words such as love, peace, joy, happiness etc. Every time you pick up the bottle and read these words you will transfer these vibration into the water. Swirling water in your glass prior to drinking, like a tornado, is said to also increase the positive vibration of the water also.

Self-love as Fuel

Self-love is action. It is the fuel which drives us to go out and get what the soul needs for deep fulfillment. Many people however are motivated by fear and not being good enough. So, they set out to achieve and succeed to give themselves a sense of worth. But they have got this backwards. We don't need to do anything to be loved and worthy. Many people confuse their egotistical needs with the needs of the true self.

For instance, experiencing intimacy through romantic relationships is something which can help the soul to grow and develop through the sharing of oneself with another. However, many people seek love from a feeling of lack. They feel they need someone to affirm they have worth and value. Instead we should find our worth first and then look for relationship to help us and the other to grow further through love.

When we have sufficient self-love, we develop a positive aggression and drive to go out and claim what our hearts desires. This type of aggression is healthy and is used as a form of fuel to drive us, as opposed to harming or hurting others. Love is the only fuel and energy we need to live life to the fullest. Once we connect with it, we discover that the supply is limitless. This is the cornerstone of true success and fulfillment.

The Unempathic Empath

Some of you may be left feeling confused to find a chapter on Narcissism in a book such as this. I would like to say that this is a touchy subject for some people. The type of narcissism which is being discussed here is called covert narcissism, not the traditional overt narcissism kind which we are more commonly aware of.

The fact is that some Empaths can become narcissists, but the covert type. This is something which I have witnessed in a number of my clients hence the reason for this chapter. If you're an empath who has been subject to attacks from Narcissists in the past, then please try to keep an open mind reading this chapter. I believe it will help you to handle any such people better in future.

Narcissism has long been defined as a personality disorder (PD). People who have PD's develop behaviors and traits which cause them to act in distressing ways to others. This prevents them from functioning adequately in their relationships. This can be seen in both their private and social lives.

Narcissism (NPD) is a personality disorder where the sufferer develops a heightened sense of themselves. They come across as arrogant, pretentious, selfish and controlling. They will often do whatever they can to be in control through a fake sense of entitlement and a heightened sense of importance. The narcissist cannot bare to be without control so will therefore do whatever they can to grasp it.

NPD develops when the spilt which is created when the child is born, is too painful for the child to bare. So, the child then takes on a grandiose false self, to make themselves feel better. From this false self-creation, they develop the belief that they are more special than others. The NPD character is generally seen to develop in dysfunctional family systems.

Narcissists usually struggle to handle criticism because they hold onto deep unresolved feelings of shame, guilt, vulnerability and fear. They try to cover up these hurtful feelings with an exaggerated sense of importance.

An increasing number of empaths have been seen to take on a different form of NPD which is known as Covert Narcissism. This type of Narcissist is usually sensitive and vulnerable, which makes them behave in defensive, hostile and introverted ways. Its roots are similar to the general form of NPD. But the behaviors are somewhat different. Coverts still possess grandiose fantasies. But as they are usually sensitive, they are not comfortable outwardly expressing their heightened importance as they can feel that others wouldn't be accepting of them. The covert is usually characterized by worry, anxiety, vulnerability, unfilled dreams and expectations. The covert will harbor grandiose, inflated and self-centered fantasies. Covert empaths often believe that they are 'special' because they have been blessed with empathic gifts. This fuels their belief and inflated sense of self. They will often see themselves as heroes who should be overachieving and can sometimes become the center of attention. But it is their empathic abilities and their naturally high vibration which makes them stand out.

The coverts often believe they are special or different from others and that no-one understands them. They may convince themselves that they feel this way because they have a special purpose in life. Self-obsession - the covert will become caught up in their own little world.

Because of their introversion and sensitivity, they go further into themselves where these unrealistic dreams of achievement plague their minds. Everything which happens to them, they believe is by divine presence. The problem with these grandiose dreams is that they are not matched with dedication and efficacy to do the work to achieve them. These people end up conflicted within themselves, on one hand they have overwhelming dreams but on the other hand they are too sensitive and afraid to pursue them. This defensiveness causes them to repress any qualities they possess which could help them move forward in their lives. They are in conflict with themselves. On one hand, they feel highly important but on the other they see these grandiose desires as unacceptable, which makes them feel guilty.

Their conscience also detects these self-grandiose ideas are trying to take all the power and positivity for oneself by withholding from others. For that reason, the covert narcissist will often be full of envy when they witness other people doing well. Although they still have the ability to sense and feel others, this is overcome by their own need to succeed, to fill the void in themselves. The pain they carry hurts them deeply, therefore they do whatever they can to avoid feeling it.

Although the 'regular' narcissist (overt) also carries deep pain within, the coverts natural sensitivity, makes the pain feel so much worse. To the outside world, the covert narcissist comes across as shy, passive, nice and even friendly. They are usually introverted and modest. But inside the covert is unconsciously trying to find a means to control others. This is often done in very subtle ways, which usually go unnoticed.

Childhood grandiosity which developed as a means of safety makes its way into adulthood. But just as we do in childhood, we don't take the action required to achieve. We just have dreams. The covert believes on some level that the universe is conspiring to bring huge success and happiness into their lives. The sad thing about this, is that coverts are usually very talented but fall into these false feelings of grandiosity which prevent them from taking mature responsibility to use their talents and gifts. As they carry unrealistic fantasies and goals into adulthood they are also usually perfectionists because of this, their standards and dreams are so high, that the covert usually fails to act as nothing could ever meet their unrealistic standards. This unfortunately reinforces feelings of low self-esteem and worthlessness because no action towards this high ideal is ever taken. As a result, coverts can also fall into depression if they fail to move towards their magnificent dreams and visions.

Childhood feelings of shame accompany the covert because they fail to act on their goals and because they even dared to envision these high ideals for themselves. Their dreams do not match their low self-esteem. They may never even be able accomplish smaller goals which further increases their lack of self-worth.

Although the covert empath will possess a sense of specialness, just like the regular Narcissist, the empath is instead overcome with feelings of self-doubt and doesn't have what it takes to look for validation from others. It is because of this behavior that makes coverts go under the radar unnoticed and not be seen as a direct threat by others. Coverts can also struggle with making friends or finding a romantic partner out of fear of being found out as worthless. Instead they may end up living their lives alone and in isolation, still harboring grand dreams but failing to take action toward them. They may pluck up the courage to begin, but each time their effort fails. Instead they usually end up with associates and friends who are somewhat inferior to themselves who can be controlled. This reinforces the coverts sense of grandiosity. Sometimes the covert may even believe that they are rescuing their lesser friends. They may also believe their friends and others don't see their true worth and hold onto this as resentment.

Coverts tend to have a demeaning inner voice. They talk to themselves in a belittling manner which reflects their lack of self-worth. Often times they are totally unaware of this inner chatter. They will also give attention and adore others who have achieved some success that they wish they had for themselves, but deep inside hold resentment and envy. If the covert does do excellent work, they will often be afraid of showing their achievements to others so will rarely receive any real validation. They also tend to be procrastinators over things which are well within their competences because deep down their low self-worth conflicts with them achieving their goals. They are against themselves due to their huge ideals and low self-worth.

How can someone with such little value be so deserving of success and achievement? This spilt haunts them for most of their lives unless they can seek help to resolve this issue before life passes them by.

Overcoming Covert Behavior

The first step is to begin seeing the reality of life. Nothing happens unless one takes action. The universe is not conspiring for us to live our dreams and be lazy at the same time. This is irrational child-like thinking. The mature responsible adult knows, that if they're to achieve anything they must do so through action.

Taking full responsibility for life helps bring the covert back to reality. A lack of responsibility leads into a cycle of continual failure and immaturity. By failing to take action, they don't move forward, which keeps their low self-worth stuck.

The covert should start to write and set achievable goals for themselves and begin working towards them. Through action, belief and dedication they will gradually begin to achieve these goals. This will slowly begin to salvage and repair their self-worth from the depths of their pain. With every accomplishment, they will begin to realize that they can trust in themselves. By fully committing, their life will begin to transform as their self-love grows.

But this can only come through hard work and a willingness to look at themselves for what they really are. To look at oneself as an insignificant human in this game of life. Only by reaching this low point of genuine humility can we begin to build ourselves back up, in the right way.

By learning to detach from ourselves, we can see who we are from an outside perspective. How do others see us? How would a friend see us? Or a family member? This type of insight can be incredibly powerful in helping to promote change. Once we can detach and look at ourselves and our character objectively we see things which we didn't see before, and gradually we can begin to release the parts that do not serve us. But also recognize our inherent worth.

Becoming Empathic

Coverts believe that they are kind, sensitive and caring people. Yes, they are in touch with their natural empathy but it has been wired up the wrong way. Instead coverts use their heightened sensitivity to try and subtly control others. They will find it easy to befriend those who are passive and so they can get their wounded emotional needs met. The covert is usually scared of strong dominant characters because they feel threatened by them, as they know they cannot control these people.

Coverts can't empathize with others in a healthy way either, they may feel others pain but will usually put their own needs first. This all occurs unconsciously, and the covert has no idea that their behavior is subtly exploitative of others. The good news is that the 'unempathic empath' can turn this around to become genuinely more empathic.

One of the biggest dangers of being an empath is that we automatically assume we are nice and caring. That we can feel genuine concern for others. The covert empath believes that they are at the mercy of other people's feelings because they can sense them so deeply, so not wanting to feel powerless they learn to protect themselves in an unhealthy way which leads to a lack of authentic understanding and compassion of others.

Many coverts can become obsessed with self-development or healing themselves. They become relentless in this pursuit. However, this simply reinforces their self obsession. They may also use suffering as a means of gaining sympathy from others and as a way of controlling or manipulating. These tactics are incredibly subtle. Coverts are usually quite rigid in their ways of doing things and find it difficult to take advice or criticism. All empaths have the ability to sense and feel but some can struggle to display genuine traits of empathy such as unconditional acceptance, forgiveness and complete understanding of another. Their empathic gift is still stuck in an immature phase.

The Empath, Stress and Cortisol

Empaths are naturally more prone to suffering stress and anxiety due to their sensitivity. But have you ever wondered what makes us feel so overwhelmed and if there are ways in which we can handle these symptoms better? This chapter will look to explore the relationship between being an empath with the natural stress response of humans.

Neurological research has shown that a part of the brain called the Amygdala is highly sensitized in empaths when compared to their non-sensitive counterparts. This part of the brain becomes easily stimulated in empaths during situations that incite an emotional response such as anxiety or stress. The Amygdala is an almond shaped group of neurons which are located within the brains temporal lobe. The main function of the Amygdala is to help us process emotions. It is also linked to the fear and pleasure responses. The more overwhelming an emotion is, the more the Amygdala responds, through this mechanism it directly controls the fight or flight response and the associated hormones. Dr. Elaine Aron who conducted the research discovered that when empaths were shown imagery of human suffering, their brains naturally responded to activate the amygdala which flooded the system with the stress hormones - cortisol, adrenaline and norepinephrine.

Empaths are more likely to suffer from anxiety and stress, conditions which activate the Amygdala into triggering the adrenal glands to release the stress hormones. These hormones in excess are particularly harmful to the human body and have been linked to stroke, heart disease and high blood pressure. Excessive release of the stress hormones can also lead to adrenal burnout. The adrenal glands are situated in the kidney region of the body and this is where the stress hormones are secreted from.

Unfortunately for us, the amygdala is not a part of the brain we can control. It is not related to our conscious thinking. It works in reaction when submitted to stress, fear or other emotions. The stress response in and of itself is not bad, we need this natural reaction to survive as humans. If we are presented by a real danger these hormones help us function more efficiently by increasing our energy and strength. However, when over-stimulated, they become harmful to our well-being and health. The main stress hormones, cortisol and adrenaline, increase heart rate and glucose levels for energy. These are needed in a threatening situation. But when these hormones are continuously being activated by non-threating circumstances (such as in generalized anxiety), they become harmful.

Empaths are easily over stimulated by things others do not find particularly stressful. So, we tend to over secrete these hormones which leads to Adrenal fatigue which can then impact the body's ability to produce these hormones in sufficient quantity to meet the demands of over stimulation. In the end the empath can become ill, unhappy, stressed or anxious. This reaction is further compounded, by the fact that empaths don't need to be directly involved in a stressful situation to invoke the stress response. The stress response can be stimulated from simply being in the presence of others or a busy environment. Being in the company of another while they're suffering has the power to trigger the stress hormones in the empath.

The nervous system is comprised of two parts, the Sympathetic and the Para-Sympathetic nervous system. The sympathetic part controls heart rate, blood pressure, digestion etc, these are the parts which run automatically and which we have little control over. The para-sympathetic nervous system on the other hand, controls sexual arousal, urination and salivation. Breathing falls under the influence of both parts of the nervous system. It happens automatically but we can also take control of it.

For 'normal' or less sensitive people, once an overwhelming or stressful situation has passed, their stress levels reduce to normal and the amygdala stops reacting. But for empaths this stress response can become a constant companion. This in turn prevents them from functioning at their best and increases the risk of health complications.

Here we will explore various methods to calm down the over sensitized nervous system, so it isn't as easily triggered. If you can get a handle on this, you can gradually reduce anxiety and heal the nervous system. If you do suffer from anxiety then nervous system exhaustion is a very real problem. But if it is dealt with, the sensitive can live life with more ease. By promoting relaxation, we can calm the body and anxiety will naturally reduce as a result.

In anxious, stressed or depressed individuals, the nervous system will usually be running autonomously via the Sympathetic response mechanism which controls the fight, flight or freeze reactions. The 'fight or flight' response does serve a positive purpose but in the modern day we are triggered too easily. Being late for work or someone passing a negative remark our way, can cause us to release stress hormones. Of course, these experiences aren't pleasant but our sensitivity causes us to over compensate, which floods our bodies with these hormones.

In the past, this natural reaction of our brain was only experienced when we were faced with real danger. But in the modern day, we are constantly impacted by small things which create the same response within us. If you're empathic by nature and tend to get overwhelmed easily, there is a high chance you're releasing stress hormones in high quantities.

To help paint a clearer picture we can use the analogy of a car. When we are stressed or anxious and feel overwhelmed as a result, we have our foot down hard on the gas pedal. However, by learning how to control the stress, we are able to access the brake to help slow us down. Empaths need to find techniques for coping and managing their response to stress.

How to help manage stress hormones

1 - Through meditation and mindfulness we can learn to control our thoughts. By getting a handle on our thoughts we aren't as easily overcome by external situations.

2 - Stay away from environments and people who make you feel overwhelmed. These circumstances are likely to trigger the stress response and until you can learn to remain in control it is better to avoid them. This isn't always possible but do your best.

3 - Avoid unhealthy foods and eat a healthy diet. Staying away from stimulants such as caffeine or other drugs like alcohol. These prevent the system from remaining calm and in control. Certain foods contain high sugars and additives that also stimulate the stress response. Try to stick to a clean, healthy diet whenever possible.

4 - Exercise regularly to help increase feel good endorphins while helping to reducing stress hormones.

For empaths to feel calm and focused they need to leverage everything they can. Secreting stress hormones every time we get over stimulated prevents us from remaining calm and living in peace. Instead it can make us tense. Learning to relax in most situations helps the nervous system to calm which will also help reduce our over sensitivity. Learning to manage and reduce these stress hormones was a big shift in helping me to remain calmer. With regular practice, our stress response can begin to relax. I would recommend every empath explore what works best to help them unwind.

The next chapter is focused on the power of breathing techniques. Learn these methods as they also help to reduce the stress response.

Empath Breathing Techniques

With our bodies in optimal condition we can fully embrace, and express our empathic qualities. Many of us have probably heard or read about using various breathing techniques to help us improve the quality of our life. The problem is that many people tend to forget about this important practice when they need it most. The art of deep breathing has been around for thousands of years and was one of the key ways people used to keep themselves calm in overwhelming situations. However, in the modern day many of us breathe much shallower which can be particularly problematic for sensitives.

The art of breathing is believed to have come from ancient India where it was first used by Yoga practitioners. The most well-known form of breathwork is called Pranayama, which means to control the life force which flows through the body. Empaths are impacted by this 'life force' of not just their own bodies, but other peoples, animals, places and even objects. Heightened sensitivity can be managed through deep breathing which essentially helps to calm the nervous system. Conscious deep breathing activates and enables the para-sympathetic nervous system to take control over the sympathetic nervous system (responsible for the fight or flight stress response). So, by healing and restoring the nervous system to optimal health, can have a positive effect on the empaths day to day functioning.

In this chapter, we will explore various techniques which can be incorporated into your daily regime in order to help manage your sensitivity and help you remain calm.

Breathing is a strange function of the body since it is voluntary and involuntary. Most of the nervous systems functions work autonomously and we have little control over them. This is what helps make breathing a powerful tool because we can take control of the nervous system by controlling the breath. Although breathing occurs automatically we can also consciously manage it whenever we wish to do so.

Research has demonstrated that deep breathing helps us to train how the body reacts to stress and external stimulus which is what makes it such a powerful tool. It does this by helping to reduce the production of stress hormones such as cortisol. Deep breathing essentially helps us to pull more oxygen into the body which helps us to function better. Here are some of the benefits associated with deep breathing.

1. Stress

An empath's brain and nervous system is usually on high alert and ready to be stimulated by any external stimulus. Deep breathing helps pull us out of a state of high stress. Conscious breathing automatically improves relaxation which is the perfect solution for keeping stress at bay.

2. Anxiety

As discussed, controlled breathing activates the parasympathetic nervous system which is linked to the Vagus nerve - this runs from the base of the brain down to the abdomen. It is involved in controlling the nervous systems responses and helps to lower heart rate. However, the Vagus nerve is also responsible for releasing a neurotransmitter known as acetylcholine which naturally promotes a sense of calmness and better focus. Acetylcholine directly works to reduce feelings of anxiety and it can also help in treating depression. Breathe deeper to stimulate the mind to release this powerful neurotransmitter.

3. Blood Pressure

Empaths are prone to having higher blood pressure due to their sensitivity. But breathing consciously can help to control and even reduce blood pressure and heart rate.

4. Brain Development

Empaths are also more likely to struggle with mental conditions such as ADD/ADHD, depression, anxiety and various other psychological conditions. However, research has discovered when deep breathing was practiced alongside a meditation practice, the size of the subject's brains could be enhanced. Through this practice, the brain was seen to develop in areas related to attention and processing of external sensory input. This can be a huge advantage for sensitives since most of their problems are related to taking in too much stimulus. Instead it may enable them to control what they allow in and process it in a more efficient manner so it isn't as over stimulating.

With deep breathing, we can begin to calm our over reactive system down. Old thought patterns, emotions and energies become stuck in the physical body but regular deep breathing helps us to clear them out. Empaths can begin to feel more connected to their reality through the art of deep breathing. Through this connection, they develop the ability to draw out what is good and learn to avoid unconscious negativity which bombards them in modern day culture. By learning to connect to the love within ourselves, through the heart, we can also begin to connect to the love all around us. This eternal ever present love, can be drawn into our physical bodies through practicing deep breathing.

Deep Breathing Methods

Most people have heard of belly breathing. This is where the abdomen expands during the inhale phase and contracts during exhalation. All deep breathing exercises are based around this notion.

The simplest act of conscious breathing begins by breathing in through the nose as deeply as you can, drawing it into your whole being. While simultaneously concentrating on breathing in love and exhaling negativity. The more you give (exhale) the more you are able to receive (inhale). This cyclic approach is one of the systems of life on Earth, it can be seen everywhere from the weather cycles to the Earth orbiting the Sun. Try to breath consciously, as often as possible or whenever you remember to. It is especially potent when dealing with stressful circumstances or whenever you feel you need to calm or relax. Conscious breathing can also help the empath to transmute negative energies into positive loving energy.

Another technique for practicing breath work, is to inhale through the nose for a count of 4, then exhale through the mouth for a count of six. Continue this rhythm for as long as you can. This method of breathwork slows down the normal respiratory rate by around half.

8/8/8 Breathing method

A popular breathing technique which I teach to my clients is called the 8/8/8 method. I recommend doing this the moment you wake up to help recharge you and get you ready for the day ahead. Then use it throughout the day whenever you feel overwhelmed.

Take 8 slow deep breathes, in through the nose and out through the nose. Then take another 8 slow breathes, but this time in through the nose and out through the mouth. Finally take another 8 deep breathes, this time in through the mouth and out through the mouth. With each out breath, visualize negative unwanted energy leaving you and during the in-breathe envision positive loving energy filling you.

Breathing deeply has been proven to positively impact the heart, brain, immune system and digestion which are all of course, related to the nervous system. This part of our physiology needs our conscious help and support to neutralize it. Breath work is simply a tool to help us remain grounded and more in control.

Breath of Fire

Breath of fire is a different technique of breathing. It is instead a rhythmic breathing technique which has been made popular by a form of Yoga known as Kundalini. Rapid breathing such as the breath of fire, can impact the sympathetic part of the nervous system, which controls our 'flight or fight' response. Since empaths go into this state frequently it can be a powerful tool to help calm and soothe them following over stimulation.

This form of breathing is different from regular deep breathing because it is much shallower, and no deeper than simply sniffing. Kundalini practitioners believe that this form of breathing is one way to experience higher consciousness. But for empaths it can help us feel more in tune with our gifts and strengths. The best time to practice this technique is whenever you feel disconnected from your power. With regular practice and commitment, you'll gradually begin to regain focus, relaxation and relieve stress or anxiety. Some people prefer this breathing technique more than deep breathing. But try to find what works best for you.

The benefits which breath of fire offers, is that it can help clear the empaths energy quickly. Due to the high levels of oxygen intake it helps to fight disease and release trapped negative energies which have been picked up or stored within the body. It can also stimulate the 3rd chakra (in the abdomen region), also known as the Solar Plexus, by helping produce heat in this region. This area is our emotional core and stores a lot of energy, by activating it through breath we can experience a boost in energy and focus. One other great benefit of this breathing technique, is that it helps us to strengthen the aura, or the magnetic field surrounding the body. This can help massively to keep unwanted negative energies and emotions out from our space. It acts as a form of psychic protection to prevent absorption of negative energies. This is all done through the balancing and strengthening impact this breathing modality has on the nervous system.

How to do the Breath of Fire

Here is a step by step explanation of how to do the Breath of Fire. Take the time to practice this regularly to notice the benefits.

1. Make yourself comfortable in a seated position. Keep your back straight and long. Rest your hands on your thighs and close your eyes while breathing normally. As

you breathe focus on your abdomen, as it moves in and out. The breath of fire is controlled by the diaphragm, which uses the solar plexus to push the navel in and out with each breath.

2. Now open your mouth wide and begin panting. Try to notice the mechanisms involved in your breathing. Try to maintain a steady rhythm of fast short breaths.

3. Close your mouth and continue this breathing pattern through your nostrils.

4. Each breath should be a quick shallow inhale and exhale with no pause between. You should be completing 2-3 breathing cycles per second.

5. Practice this for a couple of minutes at a time. Even a few short minutes will help you to feel more relaxed almost immediately.

Incorporating breathing techniques into your daily routine will help you to feel calmer and more focused. Conscious breathing should be a tool which can rely on whenever it is needed. Over long term use you will be much more grounded and unaffected by external energies as much.

Empath Supplementation & Energy Recharging

Empaths can learn to boost their physicality and health to become more robust to illness. If we don't work to protect and clear our energy regularly, we get bogged down which lowers our immune system and makes it easy for us to pick up illnesses. For empaths to remain in tip top condition they must take care of each part of their health – the mental, physical and spiritual.

As the popular saying goes 'like attracts like', the same is true with our lifestyles. If we feel bad from taking on others' emotions and energy, then we will naturally feel like eating bad unhealthy food. Alternatively, when we feel good we'll more likely eat good food. This can become a cycle, where if we feel bad, then we eat bad food and feel even worse. This cycle then continues and can be difficult to break.

My first book goes deeper into the importance of the diet and its importance for Empaths. So here we will focus more on what supplements can be introduced. You should always try to eat a healthy balanced diet and use supplements as a boost. You cannot eat a terrible diet and then expect supplements to balance this out. They don't work like this, but they can help enhance an already good diet.

Here will explore various herbs which can be used to calm the nervous system from becoming overly stimulated. Synthetic supplements and anti-psych drugs are not recommended for natural empathic healing as they play havoc with the body's natural balance. Whenever possible try to use natural supplements. Many of these herbs are often recommended for other conditions such as anxiety.

Valerian - This increases an amino acid called GABA, which works as a neurotransmitter within the central nervous system. It has a calming and soothing effect on any nervous activity and is most often used to help sensitives sleep better.

Passionflower - This too is used to help promote sleep and reduce nervousness. It also increases GABA, which is a naturally produced amino acid in the brain. It helps to reduce brain activity which promotes sleep and reduces anxiety. In the right dosage, it is a supplement the empath can take during the day providing it doesn't make them drowsy.

Scullcap - Another herb, which works directly upon the nervous system to help calm it down. It is considered a powerful medicinal supplement that has been used for many hundred years as a relaxing agent. Due to its soothing effects, it helps promote natural balance and also strengthens the nervous system and body. It can help keep the mind and psychology balanced so we can experience more positive interactions.

Kava Kava - This is best known as a nervous system relaxant. Kava Kava contains lactones which cause the nervous system to induce a muscle relaxing effect. It has been used to help with anxiety while not effecting concentration or alertness. It works by relaxing the smooth muscles. Through this relaxing, it settles the whole system down, so we can communicate effectively with others. Because of this effect it can help promote sociability. It has also been linked to improving brain function and is often used as an exercise supplement by athletes.

St.Johns Wort - This herb has been used for many years due to its calming tonic effect on the nervous system. It is commonly used to help treat depression. The best effects from this come when it is used over a longer period of time. The positive benefits are generally felt after at least 3 months of consistent use. If your energy is particularly low, St. John's wort can help gradually bring it back up. This makes it a must have for all empaths. It works by calming the nervous system while improving and strengthening it at the same time.

Exercise

A quick word on exercise, we are probably aware of the lifestyle benefits associated with regular exercise. But there is one aspect of intense exercise which has been seen to negatively impact empaths and sensitives. Extreme bouts of exercise, which require exerting a lot of effort, can over sensitize the body and over stimulate the sensitive nervous system. Intense exercise can therefore make us even more sensitive, which is something many of us do not want. Following a hard session of exercise, the empath's nervous system is over stimulated and must be calmed down afterwards, otherwise the body goes into a catabolic state where it further releases stress hormones. Exercise makes us feel great and helps clear our energy, but pay attention if you feel more sensitive following a work-out, if so then try to use some of the information described in this book to calm yourself down. This is only usually seen in excessive and intense bouts of exercise. A brisk walk or a light jog wouldn't be enough to elicit such a response.

Recharging Techniques

Empaths find it difficult to keep their energy charged. Various aspects of life such as work, family and social lives can drain us of our vital life energy which in-turn makes it easier for us to pick up unwanted energies in the process. This of course, brings our energy down even lower. This low energy state can attract energy vampires, while also making us shy away in our social and personal interactions.

Along with shielding techniques (which you can find in my first book), empaths need to find suitable ways of recharging. First and foremost, most empaths know that spending time alone is incredibly helpful but this isn't always possible, especially if we have a busy schedule and family life. But if you do have the opportunity to take some time alone, then that is probably the simplest way to recharge.

Here are some quick and easy recharging techniques you can build into your daily life to help keep your energy high and stress low.

1 - Nature

Going out into nature is an incredibly powerful way to help you recharge. It offers a simple and quick boost. If you can get to a park or a wooded area during a lunch break then that's great. But you can also reap the benefits from nature by simply walking bare foot on grass. This helps to naturally ground us to the Earth which positively impacts our energy and aura. The electromagnetic energy of the Earth helps us to clear and process negative energies we have picked up, while also helping to calm the sensitive nervous system. By combining grounding techniques with deep breathing together, you have an even more potent tool. Try to build nature into your daily routine if possible. Maybe you can take a different route to work or go for a jog in nature, instead of pounding a treadmill.

2 - Epsom Salt Bath - Epsom salt contains the vital nutrient magnesium and research has proven that this is easily absorbed by the body through the skin. Magnesium plays an important role in many bodily processes such as reliving stress, eliminating toxins, improving nerve and muscle function to name but a few. Epsom bath salts work well to help empaths release pent-up tension and stress picked up throughout the day. Bathing in Epsom salt regularly is an incredibly easy way to recharge the body's energy through detoxing.

3 - Journal - Since empaths experience such a high degree of emotion and energy they can often be left confused wondering what's theirs and what isn't. For this reason, they need to find various ways to process these emotions otherwise they become stored and stuck in their physical and energetic bodies. A great way to 'dump' this unwanted energy is to journal at the end of each day and write about what you have been feeling. This doesn't involve any criticizing or judging but simply sensing and expressing yourself. Getting into the habit of releasing and processing emotions will help you to feel more powerful as an empath each and every day.

It is easy for empaths to get lost in the feelings of external emotions and energies. But by learning and incorporating these easy exercises into their daily routine they can learn to live each day from their power. When we take care of our energy, it booms outward and if it is clear and positive, we attract the same back to us.

How to Access Your Truest Self

The last chapter of this book has been written to help each one of us to connect with our essence. Through this we can learn to live in our power. At the very core of who you are is Love. This is the center of each and every one of us. The problem is that this part of ourselves gets blocked out and covered up through the pains and hurts we experience. In response, we create a shell around ourselves to protect this delicate core. But once we can connect with this truth again, our inner and outer worlds begin to open up which synchronically brings more good and love to us.

'Liberation of the core self depends on ego strength. An overwhelmed ego defends itself for as long as it can and then yields. Only when self-defensive anxieties, impulses and wishes have been significantly resolved can the ego surrender itself to the true core self, with its firm but fluid boundaries between self and the other. The core self is not a dark and seething cauldron but a lively seeker of an intimate connection.'

- Love Outraged and the Liberation of the Core Self by Franklin Sollars

Spirituality teaches us that the spirit or soul is our truest and most authentic self. But as we have discussed in previous chapters, we can become disconnected from this aspect of ourselves. Following the split from unconscious oneness and love, if we are fortunate to have received positive parenting in a loving environment then we can develop still maintaining a connection to the authentic self.

Therefore, if our connection to love is reinforced in a positive loving atmosphere, this allows the child to grow up with a healthy self-esteem and confidence, which are considered the prerequisites to a successful and happy life. If however, upon experiencing the spilt from oneness the child's environment is hostile and they experience emotional trauma then the spilt creates further distance away from the unconditional love they had originally felt. When this separation is too much we develop a false self, which solidifies the distance from the authentic self. This person then grow ups not knowing who they are. They may learn to develop a fake sense of confidence and add numerous attributes to their false self. But all of this only strengthens the false-self's hold over the authentic repressed self.

The good news is that whatever skills and attributes were learned and developed within the false Self, they're not forgotten. Upon identifying with our inherent truth, these skills can be transferred onto the authentic self. Nothing is lost, yet all is enhanced in this situation.

We should try to understand how we can get more in touch with our deepest nature to heal and live happier. Everyone's true self has common qualities. Whether we nurture and develop these attributes or not, either way they are always there but lie dormant if not used. If we choose not to pay these attributes much attention we may become sick and tired of life while invariably functioning way below our potential. In fact, our natural qualities act as a vehicle to help us bring our gifts and talents out into the world.

Repressing Emotions

Our emotions are powerful messengers which allow us to know ourselves more. The problem is that people tend to use them as an indicator of how external situations or other people are making them feel. But instead it is our true self trying to communicate something to us. So instead of repressing our emotions we need to feel them without judgement. Unfortunately, most of us are guilty of repressing certain emotions and the amount of psychological energy required to do this is incredibly high. This is a waste of our energy and we end up repressing positive good emotions along with the unwanted ones. If we are able to reclaim this energy we can become more productive, less tired and have more peace of mind. By not suppressing certain emotions we learn more about our true self. When we repress things, we repress parts of our truth at the same time.

All emotions carry a unique energy, so when we feel either our own or someone else's, this emotional energy fills our aura and colors our experience either positively or negatively. Our emotions are here to teach and guide us, once we can become aware of this, we can stop running from or suppressing them.

Here we will explore some important things we can get do to helps us get deeper in touch with our truest self -

1) Love

Love is the core. Before we come to the realization that we are separate, we are surrounded by a feeling of unconditional love and complete oneness.

Love is the most powerful source in the universe. Between humans it offers care, passion, intimacy and connection. Everyone is on the lookout for love because it allows us to feel ourselves most deeply through physical, emotional and spiritual connection. Searching for the unconditional love we felt as babies, is what drives us to seek out romantic love and to be loved by others. When we know, and recognize that our deepest self is love, this allows us to attract more of it into our lives. It opens us up for healthy intimacy, letting us love and be loved.

Genuine intimacy permits us to engage our deepest self and form an authentic connection with the other's deep self. It is the God self in each of us connecting with one another. Love is often considered as one of life's most fulfilling experiences and for that reason it also contains the most pain. Real love first begins with oneself. We must learn to cultivate it by getting more in tune with it. Once we can begin to harness and truly feel the love within, then life and our world begins to open up as we become rooted in our deepest self.

If you have been wounded or deeply hurt, you may have lost touch with love. Only by loving yourself unconditionally can you extend it to others. Then you are comfortable opening the doors of your Self to others. Many feel vulnerable when exposing themselves in intimate relationships, but if they feel the same vulnerability from the other, then together they can let go of any defenses and both gain access to their own truth and one another's. True love is the ability to see what is real and authentic within the other.

Loving Meditation

A technique to help us get more in touch with our authentic loving nature, is to practice a loving meditation. This involves thinking of someone or something you love deeply. This can either be a partner, a child, a family member or even a passion of yours. Close your eyes and concentrate on the feelings of love that this person evokes in you. Also concentrate on where you feel it most in your body. Love is usually sensed the strongest in the heart area.

Try to remain with the feeling of love and allow it to grow and expand throughout your entire body. Meditate for as long as you can remain with these sensations of love. Gradually, overtime you will start to become more connected to yourself.

2) Creativity

'a great artist is but a conduit for an expression that resonates with something that is greater than him or herself'

- Imaginary Foundation

True creativity is the idea that something bigger than each one of us has found an outlet through us. Therefore, it is not something which belongs to us. It is simply an expression of a greater source of power. Essentially what we do through creativity transcribes what is coming through us, into an external form. This allows each of us a unique expression of this inner form. It can be seen as a God force, since we have the ability to develop and manifest our ideas into form, just as the whole of creation unfolded. We can shape ourselves and our world into what we want to see. When this comes from a deep connection with our truest self then creativity becomes almost effortless. We can even go into a flow state where we work gracefully and at ease while producing our best work. Creativity enables us to learn new skills which helps us to learn more about ourselves and strengthens the connection to our deep identity.

Through creating we tap into our potential and open the door to new possibilities. It allows us to access our own individuality and nature, then with practice we can express deeper and deeper aspects of ourselves. This is how the best pieces of music and the arts are created.

Since we create from within, what we produce is a unique expression of love. It is a part of universal energy shining through the lens of ourselves, out into the physical world. Each one of us is a unique lens which reflects this energy in various ways. It allows us to be individual but stay connected at the same time. What we create and how well we do it, is a reflection of our self-worth. Our work or creativity doesn't need to be acclaimed worldwide to have value. If it touches us deeply, it will be healing and affirming.

Try to get more in touch with your own creativity. Grab some paints and try painting. Allow whatever is in you, to flow outward. With regular practice, you will begin to find the sweet spot of your creativity. You can also explore your natural interests and abilities. Maybe you enjoy public speaking? Drawing? Painting? Photography? Or editing video? Whatever it may be, your creativity can be expressed by any means which suits your talents best.

3) Spontaneity

Natural spontaneity is an inherent characteristic of children. They possess an inquisitiveness which allows them to act and live freely. Being truly spontaneous means we are able be ourselves fully with no interruption. This attribute develops and grows in childhood providing we are made to feel loved and wanted. We can then feel comfortable in our own skin and learn to express ourselves more. Spontaneity is fresh, it is exciting. When someone is being spontaneous it gives their personality a magnetic charm which attracts others toward them. These people naturally embrace joy and find excitement in the littlest things, just as children do. Because of this natural tendency, they are less concerned with what other people think about them and consequently others are drawn to them.

By taking our childhood spontaneity into adulthood we stay in touch with our youthfulness and innocence. This attribute also connects us to our confidence, courage, maturity and a readiness to heal. Only through expressing our feelings through such acts do we access our full range of emotions. Spontaneity therefore is the sign of someone who is deeply in touch with themselves. To understand your own spontaneity, you can ask yourself some simple questions.

What emotions do you feel most often? Do you feel like you access the full range of emotions?

How eager are you about trying new things?

How enthusiastic and excited are you by life? Do you waste time?

Do you live in the moment? Or are you always worrying about past or future events?

The answers to these questions should help you realize how you live life. Although it can be difficult at first for empaths to live more spontaneously, it is something which can be worked on.

4) Mindfulness

Another important practice to help us fully experience ourselves is through the art of Mindfulness. This is a relatively straight forward Eastern meditation practice which has recently become very popular in the West.

A traditional meditation involves sitting in silence, focusing on the breath while observing any thoughts as and when they arise. With practice and commitment eventually we learn to let go of our thoughts and the emotions attached to them. This puts us into a powerful state of detachment where we become clearer in our thinking. You also see that most of the thoughts you have throughout the day are mostly unconscious and don't serve much of a purpose except that your mind is running in automatic mode. Meditation allows us to begin taking control back over the mind and as a result negative thoughts begin to lose their hold over us.

Mindfulness is a form of active meditation. Where instead of placing all of our awareness inward we instead focus it completely into the present moment. This involves paying more attention to our thoughts, feelings and to what is going on around us. This has been proven to positively impact mental well-being while enabling us to experience our true selves more fully. It means recognizing what is occurring within us and outside of us in each moment simultaneously. Through this practice, we detach from our constant thoughts and find a sense of peace in whatever we are doing at that moment.

Through observation we can learn to detach from negativity and not allow it to overcome us. When we are not living mindfully we get too caught up in our heads by over thinking pointless thoughts. This is even more common in empaths who have to endure distraction from the external energies and emotions they are constantly feeling. This stops us noticing what is happening in the moment. We can get caught up in emotion in everyday life from a comment someone passes or when someone annoys us while driving. We lose our senses, become overwhelmed and even angry. These unconscious reactions can completely take over us.

Through mindfulness we start to notice how our thoughts are driving our behavior and emotions. By reconnecting to our bodies and paying attention to how we feel, we get more in tune with our true self and recognize when our emotions are getting the better of us.

When we are mindful we are not critical. We take whatever happens in our stride. We make no judgements on our experiences. They come and they go. Instead this allows us to appreciate ourselves and each moment more. It allows us to catch our thoughts before they spiral out of control. Then we can face them from a loving place. The long-term changes associated in living in such a way can include reduced stress, depression and anxiety while also increasing happiness and well-being. Without the mental fog of negative thoughts, we are more open to our creativity and accepting of others.

Mindfulness is a door way to the true self. You will notice little things about yourself which you weren't aware of before because you pay more attention to yourself. Or you recognize a negative part of your behavior which you hadn't observed before. This enables you to find out more about who you are.

How to be mindful

Look for ways to remind yourself to pay attention to your feelings, emotions and thoughts. Notice the little things, such as the taste of the food you eat, how you feel when you're around certain people. Through these minor tasks, we begin to pull our awareness back into the present and simultaneously experience our true self.

You can also build mindfulness into your daily life by making it regular practice. Pick a time of day when you will concentrate on being present. This can be in the morning, on the way to work, during exercise or whenever you find it easy to incorporate it into your daily routine. The trick is to stick to it.

Another tip is to try doing something new. Whenever we do something new we are naturally more alert and aware. This doesn't have to be important things. You can try a different food or start a conversation with a stranger. Whatever it is, by remaining present, you'll be protected from being overwhelmed.

Gradually you will begin to acknowledge new things about yourself. Such as behaviors, talents and abilities. These can often be easily forgotten, but one way to remember any new aspects is to name it. Even if it is something negative such as anxiety or stress. By naming them we become more aware of them and learn to handle them better.

Conclusion

Once we come to fully embrace this gift we have been bestowed with, we learn how to use our empathic intelligence to heal and develop. This book has aimed to help empaths heal from their deepest emotional wounds, so they can finally move forward to live the life of their dreams and become the people they have always dreamt of becoming.

The pain of our pasts stays with us and becomes a heavy burden which we carry around with us. Unfortunately, we cannot go around the pain but instead we have to go through it. But with faith and a desire to heal we can do this. Empaths are here to make a difference in the world, especially during the most difficult times. Build the various techniques outlined into your daily life, to help you manage your gift.

Only by healing our pain can we step into our true power. You will know when you reach this point, you will have a willingness and a desire to do things. You will naturally attract more good into your life and will experience healthier relationships. As an empath, you will have an inner knowing of the changes taking place within you. Trust in the healing process and believe that you're being strengthened for what is coming – the most exciting part of your life. I pray that you find your true self and go on to live the life which you have always envisioned for yourself.

Thank you!

If this book has helped you in any way a honest review on Amazon is always appreciated.

P.S – Download my free accompanying Emotional Healing meditation here

References

1.   http://www.unityofwalnutcreek.com/light-and-love-core-your-being

2. bigthink.com/hybrid.../an-interview-with-the-director-of-the-imaginary-foundation

3. Love Outraged and the Liberation of the Core Self by Franklin Sollars

4. The Way of Human, Volume II: The False Core and the False Self, the Quantum Psychology Notebooks (Way of the Human; The Quantum Psychology Notebooks)

46944508R00138

Made in the USA
Middletown, DE
12 August 2017